Illuminating the Path

Giulio Veglio

Illuminating the Path

Introduction

Welcome, dear reader, to a journey of enlightenment and understanding. This book, *Illuminating the Path,* is more than just a guide; it's a shared exploration into the deep and often misunderstood teachings of Jesus Christ, as recounted by Matthew, one of His closest followers. As you turn these pages, you embark on a quest not just to read but to experience and internalize the profound messages that have shaped the course of history and human spirituality.

The Purpose of This Book

This book is born from a personal quest for understanding. Like many of you, I've often found myself lost in the intricate parables and teachings of Jesus. *The Bible*, while a sacred and historical document, can sometimes feel like a maze of metaphors and riddles, especially when it comes to understanding the depth of Jesus's words. The purpose here is to decipher these teachings, breaking them down into understandable, relatable, and applicable lessons.

The Reason for Writing

My journey began as a personal endeavor. I sought to understand the teachings of Jesus for myself, to explore deeper into my faith and to comprehend the profound love and sacrifice that underscores His message. But as I walked this path, I realized that my journey could light the way for others who share similar struggles and aspirations. This book is for all who yearn to learn, understand, and develop a deeper, more intimate connection with their faith.

The Core of Our Exploration

At the heart of Jesus's teachings is His unconditional love for humanity and His desire to reconcile us with God's will. He came to console, teach, and ultimately sacrifice Himself, paying the ultimate price for our sins. Understanding these teachings isn't just about reading words; it's about embracing a way of life that honors His sacrifice and reflects His love in our daily actions and decisions.

What You Will Discover

Clarity

Each parable and teaching from Matthew's writings will be explored and explained in a manner that's both insightful and accessible.

Context

Understand the historical, cultural, and theological context of Jesus's time to appreciate the depth of His words fully.

Connection

Learn how these ancient teachings can have a profound and personal impact on your modern life, guiding your decisions and interactions.

The Invitation

Illuminating the Path is an invitation to all — whether you're a seeker, a believer struggling to understand, or simply curious about the teachings of Jesus. This book doesn't claim to have all the answers but rather seeks to be a companion in your journey of faith, offering interpretations supported by theologians and encouraging your personal reflection and understanding.

As we embark on this journey together, let's open our hearts to the teachings that have offered hope, guidance, and transformation to countless lives throughout the centuries. Here's to finding clarity, embracing love, and walking the path that Jesus laid out for us with faith and purpose.

Welcome to *Illuminating the Path*.

Contents

Introduction 3

About the Author 10

Chapter 1 – A Tale of Unthinkable Promises 12

Chapter 2 – Baptism, Wilderness and the Unyielding Mission 15

Chapter 3 – The Sermon on the Mount: The Beatitudes and Their Echoes in Our Lives 18

Chapter 4 – The Essence of Influence: Salt and Light 23

Chapter 5 – The Continuity of Conviction: Fulfilling the Law 26

Chapter 6 – Beyond the Letter: The Heart of the Matter.............. 30

Chapter 7 – The Vision of Virtue: Understanding Adultery 33

Chapter 8 – The Sanctity of Marriage: Navigating Divorce............ 36

Chapter 9 – The Integrity of Words: Understanding Oaths........... 39

Chapter 10 – The Path of Non-Retaliation: Understanding 'Eye for Eye' 42

Chapter 11 – The Boundless Horizon of Love: Understanding 'Love Your Enemies'.. 45

Chapter 12 – The Grace of Giving: Understanding 'Give to the Needy' 48

Chapter 13 – The Heart of Conversation: Understanding Prayer... 51

Chapter 14 – The Inner Sanctum of Sacrifice: Understanding Fasting 54

Chapter 15 – The Eternal Investment: Understanding 'Treasures in

Heaven'... 57

Chapter 16 – The Serenity of Surrender: Understanding 'Do Not Worry'... 60

Chapter 17 – The Mirror of Judgment: Understanding 'Judging Others'... 63

Chapter 18 – The Door of Persistence: Understanding 'Ask, Seek, Knock'.. 66

Chapter 19 – The Path Less Traveled: Understanding 'The Narrow and Wide Gates' 69

Chapter 20 – Foundations of Life: Understanding 'The Wise and Foolish Builders' 72

Chapter 21 – Discerning the Authentic: Understanding 'True and False Prophets' 75

Chapter 22 – Essence Over Appearance: Understanding 'True and False Disciples'... 78

Chapter 23 – The Conclusion of the Sermon on the Mount........... 81

Part two.. 84

Chapter 24 – Compassion in Action: Understanding Jesus' Healing of the Leper 86

Chapter 25 – The Power of Unseen Faith: Understanding 'The Faith of the Centurion' 89

Chapter 26 – The Price and Privilege: Understanding 'The Cost of Following Jesus'... 92

Chapter 27 – The Master of the Seas: Understanding 'Jesus Calms the Storm' 95

Chapter 28 – The Authority of a Single Word: Understanding 'Jesus Heals the Demon-Possessed' 98

Chapter 29 – The Authority to Forgive: Understanding 'Jesus Forgives and Heals a Paralyzed Man' 101

Chapter 30 – The Physician for the Soul: Understanding 'It is not the healthy who need a doctor, but the sick' 104

Chapter 31 – New Wine into New Wineskins: Understanding 'The Bridegroom, Fasting, and Change' 107

Chapter 32 – The Mission of the Twelve: Understanding 'The Instructions to the Disciples' 110

Chapter 33 – Jesus and John the Baptist 116

Chapter 34 – The Call to Repentance: Understanding 'Woe to Unrepentant Towns' 120

Chapter 35 – The Gentle Mastery of Christ: Understanding 'The Father Revealed in the Son' 123

Chapter 36 – The Lord of the Sabbath: Understanding Compassion Over Ceremony 127

Chapter 37 – Integrity of the Kingdom: Understanding 'God's Chosen Servant' 130

Chapter 38 – The Sign of Jonah: Understanding a Call for Repentance 134

Chapter 39 – The Parable of the Sower: Understanding the Receptivity of Our Hearts 137

Chapter 40 – The Purpose of Parables: Gaining Insight into the Kingdom 140

Chapter 41 – The Parable of the Weeds: Understanding Coexistence and Judgment... 145

Chapter 42 – The Parables of the Mustard Seed and Yeast: Symbols of Growth and Influence 148

Chapter 43 – The Parables of the Hidden Treasure and the Pearl: Discovering Incomparable Value 151

Chapter 44 – The Parable of the Net: Understanding Final Judgment and Response 154

Chapter 45 – Understanding "That Which Defiles" 158

Chapter 46 – Understanding Jesus' Prediction of His Death 162

Chapter 47 – The Kingdom of Heaven: Understanding Humility and Responsibility 165

Chapter 48 – The Parable of the Wandering Sheep: Emphasizing God's Care for the Lost.. 168

Chapter 49 – The Parable of the Unmerciful Servant: Understanding Forgiveness and Compassion 171

Chapter 50 – The Parable of the Workers in the Vineyard: Understanding God's Generosity................................... 175

Chapter 51 – The Parable of the Two Sons: Understanding Obedience and Repentance... 179

Chapter 52 – The Parable of the Tenants: Understanding Stewardship and Judgment... 182

Chapter 53 – The Parable of the Wedding Banquet: Understanding God's Invitation and Response...................................... 186

Chapter 54 – The Parable of the Ten Virgins: Understanding Preparedness and Vigilance 190

Chapter 55 – The Parable of the Bags of Gold: Understanding Stewardship and Accountability 193

Chapter 56 – The Parable of the Sheep and the Goats: Understanding Compassion and Judgment 197

Chapter 57 – Conclusion of the Parables and Transition to the Passion of Christ... 201

Closing Thoughts: Gratitude and Reflection on the Journey Through Matthew's Parables................................... 203

About the Author

Giulio Veglio stands as a testament to the transformative power of leadership and service. Beginning his illustrious career with John Paul Mitchell Systems in 1984, he swiftly advanced from an enterprising salon owner to an internationally recognized educator and master stylist. His innovative approaches to customer service have propelled multiple salons and educational institutions to the forefront of the industry.

As a Harvard Business School Executive MBA graduate and a certified Maxwell Leadership Executive, Trainer, Speaker, and Coach, Veglio embodies a lifetime commitment to personal development and empowerment. He has been awarded the 2023 Outstanding Leadership Award and the 2024 Visionary Award, underscoring his significant impact on global education and business.

Veglio's influence extends beyond the boardroom and into the heart of communities through his philanthropic efforts, raising over $25M annually for varied causes. His bilingual fluency and rich cultural experiences, spanning from Italy to the US, have enriched his engagements with diverse audiences around the world.

An ordained minister and a staunch advocate against human trafficking, Veglio's life work resonates with profound empathy and a relentless drive for societal betterment. His literary contributions further this legacy with award-winning books such as "A Slap on the Back of the Head" and "Unwrapping Your Gifts." These reflect his passion for guiding others to uncover their potential.

As an Italian immigrant who embraced US citizenship with pride, Giulio Veglio continues to illuminate paths for others, whether through his stirring oration or his written words, leaving indelible marks of inspiration across continents.

Chapter 1 – A Tale of Unthinkable Promises

As we begin this journey through "Illuminating the Path," let's start by recounting the remarkable origins of Jesus. This story revolves around the profound faith of two ordinary individuals and divine intervention. Imagine a young Mary, not yet married but pledged to Joseph, a Nazarene carpenter. Mary's life takes an extraordinary turn when the angel Gabriel visits her, delivering the bewildering news of her conception through the Holy Spirit, as told in *Luke 1:26-38*.

Imagine being in Mary's position – a virgin, engaged, and suddenly facing an unimaginable reality. Now, think about Joseph. When Mary discloses her pregnancy and the divine message, his disbelief is understandable. "An angel visited you, and now you're pregnant with the Son of God? And you've been with no one?" It's a scenario that could challenge the faith of even the most steadfast believers.

However, Joseph's world takes a sudden turn when he experiences a visitation of his own. In his dream, an angel reassures him, stating, "Joseph, son of David, do not be afraid to take Mary home as your wife because what is conceived in her is from the Holy Spirit. She will give birth to a son, and you are to give him the name Jesus because he will save his people from their sins" (Matthew 1:18-25). This revelation becomes a pivotal moment for Joseph. He chooses to embrace the message with profound faith, taking Mary as his wife and committing himself to protect her and the unborn child from any threat, including King Herod's ominous intentions.

After their marriage, Joseph remains true to his vow, to not consummate their union till the birth of Jesus. This child, born in a humble Bethlehem manger and celebrated every December 25th, would go on to lead an extraordinary life. His journey begins with a seemingly ordinary childhood, culminating in a transformative encounter with John the Baptist that sets him on his divine mission.

Let's take a moment to reflect on the significant points of faith in this narrative:

Key Points

1. **Mary's Acceptance**
   Faced with an unfathomable future, Mary embraces her role, demonstrating a surrender to faith that is both humbling and inspiring.
2. **Joseph's Belief**
   Initially skeptical, Joseph's transformation into a believer and protector stands as a powerful testament to the strength of faith in the face of the inexplicable.
3. **The Birth of Jesus**
   From humble beginnings, a figure emerges who would profoundly impact the world, reminding us that greatness often originates from the most modest beginnings.
4. **The Role of Faith**
   Throughout the story, faith serves as the guiding force, driving Mary and Joseph to accept and nurture a child destined to change the course of history.

Conclusion

This chapter isn't merely a recount of historical events; it's a contemplation on the power of belief and the strength of the human spirit when confronted with the divine. It's a narrative that resonates, offering lessons on faith, courage, and the profound impact of embracing one's role in the big picture.

Theologians' Perspective

Theologians have long debated and marveled at this story, viewing it as a cornerstone of the Christian faith. They often discuss the balance between divine providence and human free will, exemplified by Mary and Joseph's acceptance of their extraordinary roles. This narrative is seen as a profound illustration of God's interaction with humanity, a testament to the idea that faith can lead to salvation and transformation.

As we conclude this chapter, let's carry forward the enduring message of faith, hope, and the power of accepting one's path, regardless of how unexpected it may be. This is just the beginning of our exploration, a first step on the path to illuminating the deeper truths and lessons embedded in these ancient stories.

Chapter 2 – Baptism, Wilderness and the Unyielding Mission

Following the miracle birth of Jesus and the early years in Chapter 1, we now turn to a defining moment in His life: the baptism by John the Baptist. This event marks the end of Jesus' private life and the beginning of His public ministry – a moment of both revelation and affirmation. As Jesus emerges from the waters of the Jordan, the heavens themselves bear witness to His identity: "This is my beloved Son, with whom I am well pleased" (Matthew 3:17). It is a pivotal instance where John the Baptist, the herald of the Messiah, passes the baton to the one destined to be the light of the world.

The serenity of this moment is soon juxtaposed with the starkness of the wilderness, where the Spirit leads Jesus to face temptation from Satan. This is not just a physical wilderness but a spiritual one, testing the very resolve of Jesus and the steadfastness of His mission. Over 40 days, Jesus fasts, prays, and faces the devil's temptations. Each of Satan's enticements—turning stones to bread, seizing worldly power, and testing God's protection— is countered not with force but with the knowledge from the Scripture and His faith.

Key Points

1. **Jesus' Baptism by John**
   A moment of divine approval and a public declaration that Jesus is the awaited Messiah.
2. **The Temptation in the Wilderness**
   40 days of fasting represents Jesus' preparation for His ministry and shows His human vulnerability and divine authority.

3. **The Refutation of Temptation**
   Jesus' responses to Satan's temptations demonstrate His deep
   understanding of Scripture and His unwavering commitment
   to His Father's will.
4. **The Steadfast Mission**
   Despite the hardships, Jesus never wavers from His path,
   setting an example of dedication to God's calling.

Theological Perspective

Theologians view Jesus' baptism as a theological fulcrum, the
moment when He is anointed for His messianic role. This baptism is
frequently interpreted as a symbol of the new covenant, representing
the cleansing of the old and the beginning of the new.

The wilderness temptation is commonly seen through the lens of
Jesus' messianic identity and His role as the new Adam. Where
Adam failed in the Garden of Eden, Jesus succeeded in the barren
desert. Theologians also point to the temptations as symbolic of the
struggles all humans face—physical needs, power, and faith—and
how Jesus triumphs over these trials serves as a blueprint for
resisting our own temptations.

Conclusion

In this chapter of "Illuminating the Path," we've traced the footsteps
of Jesus from the Jordan River to the wilderness, witnessing the
early affirmation of His identity and the strength of His purpose.
The baptism and subsequent trials in the desert are more than tales
of endurance; they are the foundation for understanding His mission
and the nature of His kingdom, which is not of this world but of the
one to come.

As we conclude, we are reminded that in our own lives, we will face moments of decision and temptation. Jesus' example provides us with the courage and strategy to stay true to our calling. With Scripture as our sword and faith as our shield, we can walk our paths with the assurance that our steps are guided by the same Spirit that led Jesus into the wilderness and back, ready to undertake His world-changing ministry.

Chapter 3 – The Sermon on the Mount: The Beatitudes and Their Echoes in Our Lives

Here, we find Jesus amidst an eager multitude, ascending a mountainside to deliver what would become one of the most profound discourses in human history – the Sermon on the Mount. Here, in Matthew 5:3-12, we see Jesus settling in as His disciples came near, ready to receive wisdom that will echo through the ages. He begins with the Beatitudes, a series of blessings that overturn worldly values, presenting a radical vision of the Kingdom of Heaven.

"Blessed are the poor in spirit, for theirs is the kingdom of Heaven. Blessed are those who mourn, for they shall be comforted. Blessed are the meek, for they shall inherit the Earth. Blessed are those who hunger and thirst for righteousness, for they shall be filled. Blessed are the merciful, for they shall obtain mercy. Blessed are the pure in heart, for they shall see God. Blessed are the peacemakers, for they shall be called children of God. Blessed are those who are persecuted for righteousness' sake, for theirs is the kingdom of Heaven. Blessed are you when others revile you and persecute you and utter all kinds of evil against you falsely on my account. Rejoice and be glad, for your reward is great in Heaven, for so they persecuted the prophets who were before you."

Let's break this down:

1. **Poor in Spirit**
   This speaks of humility, recognizing our need for God.
2. **Those Who Mourn**
   It reflects the comfort God offers in our deepest sorrows.

3. **The Meek**
    This assures that the gentle and humble will receive the Earth's riches, not by force, but through grace.
4. **Hunger and Thirst for Righteousness**
    An intense desire for justice and ethical living that God promises to satisfy.
5. **The Merciful**
    Those who offer mercy will receive it in abundance from God.
6. **Pure in Heart**
    A call to sincerity and inner purity, promising the ultimate vision of God.
7. **Peacemakers**
    They embody the reconciliation Jesus came to bring and are recognized as God's children.
8. **Persecuted for Righteousness**
    Enduring injustice for what is right aligns us with the prophets and carries the promise of Heaven.
9. **Insulted and Persecuted for Christ**
    This is the cost of discipleship, rewarded with a profound heavenly inheritance.

Jesus' message here is clear: the values of God's kingdom often contrast sharply with worldly principles. The Beatitudes are not just blessings; they are invitations to a way of life that aligns with the heart of God. They call us to a counter-cultural existence where the last are first, the humble are exalted, and the pure in heart are celebrated.

Key Points

1. **The Reversal of Expectations**
    The Beatitudes challenge societal norms, emphasizing spiritual riches over material wealth.

2. **The Promise of Comfort**
   Jesus offers consolation and hope to those who face trials and tribulations.
3. **The Call to Righteousness**
   There's a strong emphasis on justice, mercy, and peace as hallmarks of Christian living.
4. **The Assurance of Reward**
   Jesus ensures that faithfulness, even in persecution, will be rewarded in Heaven.

Conclusion

The Beatitudes present a blueprint for Christian living that is as relevant today as it was on that mountainside. They encourage us to embrace virtues like humility, mercy, and peace – virtues that transform us and, by extension, the world around us.

Exercises to Apply the Beatitudes

1. **Humility Practice**
   Spend time in daily reflection, acknowledging your dependence on God for guidance and strength.
2. **Comfort in Mourning**
   Reach out to someone who is grieving by offering a listening ear or sending a supportive note, embodying the comfort promised by Jesus.

3. **Pursuit of Justice**
   Volunteer with a local organization that advocates social justice or helps those in need.
4. **Mercy in Action**
   Practice forgiveness towards someone who has wronged you and actively seek to mend a strained relationship.
5. **Peacemaking Effort**
   Mediate a conflict, whether it's in your family, workplace, or community, to foster reconciliation.

As we explore Jesus' teachings following the gathering of His disciples, we'll see how these principles are woven throughout His ministry. The Sermon on the Mount sets the stage for a faith-filled life that is not passive but actively engaged in bringing the Kingdom of Heaven to life on Earth.

Beatitudes Theologies

The Beatitudes have been subject to extensive theological examination and interpretation. Theologians have approached them from various perspectives, each bringing a deeper understanding of their significance in Christian doctrine and ethical living.

Catholic Theology

In Catholicism, the Beatitudes are seen as the perfection of the moral law bestowed upon Moses. They transcend mere external precepts, representing attitudes of the heart that reflect the character of Jesus Himself. They are also viewed as a roadmap to Christian perfection, often interconnected with the seven virtues—both the theological (faith, hope, charity) and the cardinal (prudence, justice, temperance, fortitude).

Protestant Theology

Protestant theologians often emphasize the Beatitudes as a description of the character of people in the kingdom of God. Martin Luther, for example, saw them as a guide on how Christians should conduct themselves, illustrating the transformative impact of Christ's salvation on a believer's life.

Eastern Orthodox Theology

The Eastern Orthodox tradition emphasizes the mystic and eschatological nature of the Beatitudes, seeing them as virtues to aspire to for a deeper communion with God. They are considered steps in the spiritual ascent, with each Beatitude building upon the one before it, leading to theosis, which is a process of becoming more like God.

Liberation Theology

Liberation theology, with its focus on social justice, views the Beatitudes as a call to action against the injustices faced by the poor and the oppressed. It sees Jesus as advocating for a reversal of the social order, where those who suffer due to societal structures are given priority in God's kingdom.

Existentialist Theology

Existentialist theologians focus on the individual and authentic experience of the believer as they live out the Beatitudes. For them, the Beatitudes challenge Christians to live a life of radical authenticity and personal transformation in a world that often opposes these values.

Conclusion

Across these varied theological perspectives, there is a consensus that the Beatitudes provide a counter-cultural portrait of Christian discipleship. They are seen as both blessings and moral imperatives that guide believers to live in a way that reflects the kingdom of Heaven. The Beatitudes call for a radical reorientation of values, centering on humility, love, and a longing for righteousness that transcends earthly desires and ambitions.

Chapter 4 – The Essence of Influence: Salt and Light

In this chapter, we explore another poignant teaching of Jesus, found in Matthew 5:13-16, where He uses the metaphors of salt and light to describe the essential role of His followers in the world.

"You are the salt of the Earth. But if the salt loses its saltiness, how can it be made salty again? It is no longer good for anything, except to be thrown out and trampled underfoot. You are the light of the world. A town built on a hill cannot be hidden. Neither do people light a lamp and put it under a bowl. Instead, they put it on its stand, and it gives light to everyone in the house. In the same way, let your light shine before others, that they may see your good deeds and glorify your Father in Heaven."

Understanding the Teaching In the ancient world, salt held value not only as a flavor enhancer but also as a preservative. When Jesus tells His followers they are *the salt of the earth,*" He urges them to act as agents of preservation against moral decay and to infuse the world with the flavor of God's wisdom. However, for salt to be effective, it must retain its distinctiveness; similarly, Christians must maintain their distinctiveness from the world to exert a positive influence.

Light illuminates and reveals. By declaring His followers *the light of the world,* Jesus tells them to live in a way that brightens the darkness, guiding others and revealing the nature of God through their actions. A light is not kindled to be concealed but to be seen; thus, Christians are to live openly and righteously.

Key Points

1. **Value of Influence**
   Just as salt and light have distinctive roles, Christians are encouraged to be influential in the world.

2. **Preservation of Goodness**
   As salt preserves, so should Christians when it comes to goodness and truth in the world.
3. **Visibility of Faith**
   Faith should be apparent to others, not hidden, just as a city on a hill or a lamp on a stand is visible to all.
4. **Intention of Deeds**
   The ultimate purpose of our 'good deeds' is not self-glory but to glorify God in heaven.

Exercises to Apply From This Teaching

1. **Preserve the Good**
   Volunteer in initiatives that combat community issues like hunger or injustice, preserving the good in society.
2. **Add Flavor**
   Engage in conversations about faith or morality, respectfully adding the flavor of Christian perspective to discussions.
3. **Illuminate Your Surroundings**
   Offer help where there is a need, give encouragement where there is despair, and bring positivity to counteract negativity in your environment.
4. **Be Visible**
   Share your experiences of faith in appropriate settings, letting others see the impact of Christ in your life.
5. **Reflect the Light**
   Mentor someone younger in faith or life skills, reflecting the light of wisdom and guidance.

Conclusion

By labeling His followers as salt and light, Jesus bestows upon them both a profound identity and responsibility. They are to actively engage with the world while preserving their distinctive character as His disciples. This teaching serves as an encouragement for us not to shy away from our calling but to wholeheartedly embrace it, allowing our lives to stand as a testament to the grace we have received.

Theologians' Take

Theologians often interpret the salt and light teaching as an indication of the Christian's call to social engagement and moral distinctiveness. They propose that Christianity is not a faith of retreat or passivity but one that engages actively with society to transform and uplift it. This passage is frequently referenced in discussions about Christian ethics and the Church's role in society. Theologians encourage believers to consider how their faith informs their public life, advocating for a visible, active faith that works for the common good while directing glory to God.

Chapter 5 – The Continuity of Conviction: Fulfilling the Law

This chapter discusses another teaching from the Sermon on the Mount, where Jesus clarifies that he is not there to abolish the Jewish Law or the Prophets. The passage in question, Matthew 5:17-20, clarifies Jesus' stance on what the Law of Moses really means to all people.

"Do not think I have come to abolish the Law of the Prophets; I have not come to abolish them to fulfill them. For truly I tell you, until heaven and Earth disappear, not the smallest letter, not the least stroke of a pen, will by any means disappear from the Law until everything is accomplished. Therefore anyone who sets aside one of the least of these commands and teaches others accordingly will be called least in the kingdom of Heaven, but whoever practices and teaches these commands will be called great in the kingdom of Heaven. For tell you that unless your righteousness surpasses that of the Pharisees and the teachers of the law, you will certainly not enter the kingdom of Heaven.

Understanding the Teaching

Jesus states that His mission is not to annul the Law but to complete it. His coming represents the culmination of what the Law aimed for, embodying its principles perfectly. He emphasizes the enduring nature of the Law, insisting that not even the smallest detail will be discarded until its purpose is fully realized. Jesus summons a more profound and heartfelt commitment to God's commandments than was demonstrated by the Pharisees and teachers of the law. While the latter were recognized for their strict and showy observance of the letter of the Law, they frequently overlooked its underlying spirit.

Key Points
1. **Reverence for the Law**
   Jesus respects the Law and the Prophets. He teaches His followers to do the same.
2. **Fulfillment, Not Abolishment**
   The Law is not rendered obsolete by Jesus; instead, He brings it to completion by embodying its intent.
3. **Enduring Validity**
   The permanence of the Law is highlighted, emphasizing that its moral and ethical teachings remain relevant.
4. **Heartfelt Righteousness**
   True righteousness goes beyond legalism and is marked by genuine moral integrity.
5. **Exceeding External Piety**
   Jesus challenges His followers to surpass the Pharisees in righteousness by being sincere in their obedience to God.

Exercises to Apply This Teaching

1. **Study the Roots**
   Take your time to read the Ten Commandments and the Prophets to understand the foundation of Jesus' teachings.
2. **Reflect on Intentions**
   When making decisions, reflect not just on the actions but the intentions behind them. Aim for integrity that aligns with the spirit of the Law.
3. **Practice Sincere Faith**
   Engage in acts of worship or charity, driven not by a desire for public recognition but as a sincere expression of your faith.
4. **Teach Through Action**
   Model ethical behavior in everyday situations, showing others the Law's relevance through your conduct.
5. **Seek Deeper Understanding**

Join a Bible study or discussion group to deepen your understanding of how the Old Testament laws relate to the teachings of Jesus.

Conclusion

Jesus' declaration about the Law emphasizes the necessity of an authentic, lived-out faith that fulfills the deeper moral and spiritual principles embedded in God's commandments. This teaching prompts us to reflect on how we embody the spirit of the Law in our lives, calling us to a righteousness that originates from within and radiates outward.

Theologians' Take

Theologians have long debated the meaning of Jesus' fulfillment of the Law. Some suggest that He completes the Law's intent through His life, death, and resurrection, providing a way for humans to attain righteousness before God. Others see in His teaching an ethical continuity, where Jesus interprets the Law in a way that emphasizes its underlying principles of love, justice, and mercy. In both interpretations, there's a consensus that Jesus does not discard the Law but rather calls His followers to understand and live out its true purpose.

The Ten Commandments, as commonly presented based on the account in Exodus 20:1-17 and Deuteronomy 5:6-21, are listed as follows:

- ❖ You shall have no other gods before Me.
- ❖ You shall not make idols.
- ❖ You shall not take the name of the Lord your God in vain.
- ❖ Remember the Sabbath day, to keep it holy.
- ❖ Honor your father and your mother.
- ❖ You shall not murder.
- ❖ You shall not commit adultery.

❖ You shall not steal.
❖ You shall not bear false witness against your neighbor.
❖ You shall not covet.

Chapter 6 – Beyond the Letter: The Heart of the Matter

This chapter is about Jesus teaching anger and reconciliation. He contrasts the sixth commandment, "You shall not murder." With the concept that if you're angry with a brother or sister, you will be subjected to judgment. In Matthew 5:21-26, Jesus says,

"You have heard that it was said to the people long ago, 'You shall not murder, and anyone who murders will be subject to judgment.' But I tell you that anyone who is angry with a brother or sister will be subject to judgment. Again, anyone who says to a brother or sister, 'Raca, is answerable to the court. And anyone who says 'You fool!' will be in danger of the fire of hell. Therefore, if you are offering your gift at the altar and there remember that your brother or sister has something against you, leave your gift there in front of the altar. First go and be reconciled to them; then come and offer your gift. Settle matters quickly with your adversary who is taking you to court. Do it while you are still together on the way, or your adversary may hand you over to the judge, and the judge may hand you over to the officer, and you may be thrown into prison. Truly I tell you, you will not get out until you have paid the last penny."

Understanding the Teaching

Jesus transcends the literal prohibition of murder, highlighting that harboring anger or disdain is tantamount to the act itself in God's eyes. He uses the term Raca (an Aramaic term for contempt) to illustrate that even our words carry the weight of moral actions. Moreover, Jesus stresses the importance of reconciliation over religious rituals, urging that amends with one another take precedence over offering gifts at the altar.

Key Points

1. **Inner Turmoil Equals Outer Acts**
   Jesus equates anger with murder in God's moral accounting, teaching that the intent and thoughts behind actions are as important as the actions themselves.
2. **The Power of Words**
   Disparaging or contemptuous language towards others is akin to physical harm, reflecting a heart not aligned with God's law.
3. **Reconciliation Over Ritual**
   The urgency of reconciling with those we've wronged takes precedence over religious ceremonies.
4. **Urgency in Resolution**
   Jesus advises settling disputes quickly, which maintains harmony and prevents further conflict.
5. **Justice and Consequences**
   Unresolved issues can lead to spiritual and earthly penalties, reinforcing the need for swift reconciliation.

Exercises to Apply This Teaching

1. **Monitor Your Anger**
   When your anger rises, take a moment, breathe and ask yourself why. Address the cause calmly rather than letting it fester.
2. **Speak Kindly**
   Make a conscious effort to avoid disparaging language, even in jest, and encourage others to do the same.
3. **Prioritize Reconciliation**
   If you know someone has something against you, reach out to resolve the issue. This can be as simple as a conversation to clear the air or even a sincere apology.
4. **Practice Quick Forgiveness**
   Learn to quickly forgive and resolve your anger rather than holding a grudge.

5. **Reflect on Disputes**

   If you're in a dispute with someone, consider what steps you can take toward resolution before it escalates to the point of no return.

Conclusion

Jesus' teaching on murder goes to the heart, revealing that the spirit of the law is about cultivating attitudes and intentions that reflect God's love and justice. He invites His followers to live out the commandments not just in actions but in thoughts and words, promoting a life of peace and reconciliation.

Theologians' Take

Theologians consider this expansion of the law as an example of Jesus' radical reinterpretation of righteousness. It's not enough to refrain from the act of murder; one must also refrain from the internal and external aggression that violates the sanctity of human dignity. This teaching is often discussed in theological circles as a call to personal transformation and societal peace-making, urging Christians to live in a manner that reflects the reconciling work of Christ.

Chapter 7 – The Vision of Virtue: Understanding Adultery

In this chapter, we interpret Jesus' teachings on adultery, which is encapsulated in Matthew 5:27-30. Jesus deepens the understanding of the seventh commandment, "You shall not commit adultery," by addressing the intentions and thoughts that lead to the act.

"You have heard that it was said, 'You shall not commit adultery.' But I tell you that anyone who looks at a woman lustfully has already committed adultery with her in his heart. If your right eye causes you to stumble, gouge it out and throw it away. It is better for you to lose one part of your body than for your whole body to be thrown into hell. And if your right hand causes you to stumble, cut it off and throw it away. It is better for you to lose one part of your body than for your whole body to go into hell."

Understanding the Teaching Jesus teaches that committing adultery is not considered to be just a physical act but also to look at someone with lustful intent. These desires are considered to be sinful in God's view. Jesus uses hyperboles, advocating the removal of the eye or hand, not as a literal command but as an illustration of the seriousness with which one should avoid sinning. The emphasis is on the importance of the heart and mind's purity, not just in behavior.

Key Points

1. **Adultery of the Heart**
   The sin of adultery begins with lustful thoughts, not just the physical act.
2. **Radical Measures for Sin**
   Jesus employs drastic metaphors to emphasize the importance of avoiding sin.
3. **Purity of Heart and Mind**

True purity transcends actions; it begins within one's thoughts and intentions.

4. **Consequences of Sin**
   Jesus warns of severe spiritual consequences for sin, urging vigilance against temptation.

Exercises to Apply This Teaching

1. **Guard Your Thoughts**
   Be mindful of what you think, and if they stray, consciously bring them to something pure and edifying.
2. **Limit Temptations**
   If certain situations or media lead you to lustful thoughts, take practical steps to avoid them.
3. **Accountability**
   Have a trusted friend with whom you can be accountable regarding struggles with lust and purity.
4. **Cultivate Respect**
   Practice seeing people as whole individuals worthy of respect rather than objects of desire, emphasizing their dignity and your own integrity.
5. **Seek Forgiveness and Growth**
   If you stumble, seek forgiveness and ask for the strength to resist.

Conclusion

Jesus' exposition on adultery invites us to a life where virtue is not just an external adherence to rules but an internal alignment with God's holiness. It challenges us to evaluate our internal world - our thoughts and desires - and to take whatever steps necessary to protect our spiritual well-being.

Theologians' Take

Theologians regard Jesus' teachings on adultery as indicative of His broader ethical teachings that prioritize inner morality over outward observance. The call to purity of heart suggests that not only external actions but any internal dispositions and intentions are considered sinful. The hyperbolic language about gouging out an eye or cutting off a hand is typically interpreted as a strong rhetorical, emphasizing the seriousness with which we should treat sin. It's understood as a call to radical discipleship, where everything that hinders one's relationship with God should be forsaken.

Chapter 8 – The Sanctity of Marriage: Navigating Divorce

In this chapter, we discuss Jesus' teachings on divorce as presented in Matthew 5:31-32. Jesus addresses the issue of divorce, a topic of much debate in His time, and continues to be so today. He references the law from Deuteronomy 24:1, which allows for divorce under certain conditions and then deepens the conversation to the heart of the marital commitment.

"It has been said, 'Anyone who divorces his wife must give her a certificate of divorce.' But I tell you that anyone who divorces his wife, except for sexual immorality, makes her the victim of adultery, and anyone who marries the divorced woman commits adultery."

Understanding the Teaching

Jesus explains that the act of divorce, except in cases of sexual immorality, leads both parties to commit adultery upon entering new relationships. He emphasizes the gravity of the marriage vow and God's initial intention for marriage to be a lifelong commitment between two individuals. His teaching reveals a deep concern for the sanctity of marriage and the well-being of all involved, especially those who might be unjustly affected by divorce.

Key Points

1. **Sacredness of Marriage**
   Jesus emphasizes that marriage is a sacred covenant, and its contract should not be taken lightly.
2. **Adultery Revisited**
   He links divorce (except in cases of unfaithfulness) to adultery, showing the spiritual consequences of ending a marriage.

3. **Protection of the Vulnerable**
   Jesus' teaching also seeks to protect individuals, particularly women of that era, who were often destitute or stigmatized because of divorce.
4. **God's Original Design**
   The teaching also reflects on God's initial goal – marriage as a lifelong and faithful union.

Exercises to Apply This Teaching

1. **Reflect on Commitment**
   If you are married, spend time to reflect on your vows and commitment. Explore ways you can strengthen your relationship.
2. **Seek Counsel**
   If you're facing marital difficulties, consider counseling or guidance from a trusted faith-based counselor or pastor before making decisions.
3. **Support Systems**
   Create or find a support system for those going through the pain of divorce, offering emotional and spiritual support.
4. **Understand Scripture**
   Study the broader biblical context of marriage and divorce to understand its complexities and God's perspective on relationships.
5. **Pray for Marriages**
   Regularly pray for your own marriage and others, seeking God's guidance, protection, and blessing.

Conclusion

Jesus' teaching on divorce brings us face to face with the seriousness with which God views marriage. It urges us to reflect deeply on the commitments we make and to pursue reconciliation and healing whenever possible.

Acknowledging the complexities of broken relationships and the accompanying pain, the teaching encourages us to view marriage through the lens of sacredness and permanence.

Theologians' Take

Theologians have made several interpretations of this passage. Some believe Jesus is emphasizing the indissolubility of marriage, while others focus on the exceptions he suggests, recognizing that Jesus acknowledges the reality of broken relationships. Many agree that Jesus is elevating the discussion from legal provisions to moral and spiritual considerations.

This teaching is often seen as a critique of a culture that treated divorce too lightly, especially considering the social and economic dangers it posed to women at the time. Theologians also emphasize that while Jesus teaches about the high ideals of marriage, he also offers grace and compassion to those who have experienced the pain of divorce.

Chapter 9 – The Integrity of Words: Understanding Oaths

This chapter is all about oaths found in Matthew 5:33-37. Here, Jesus addresses the practice of making oaths, a common cultural practice in His time used to guarantee the truth of one's words.

"Again, you have heard that it was said to the people long ago, 'Do not break your oath, but fulfill to the Lord the vows you have made.' But I tell you, do not swear an oath at all: either by Heaven, for it is God's throne; or by the Earth, for it is his footstool; or by Jerusalem, for it is the city of the Great King. And do not swear by your head, for you cannot make even one hair white or black. All you need to say is simply 'Yes or No'; anything beyond this comes from the evil one."

Understanding the Teaching: Jesus challenges His listeners to embody such honesty and integrity that oaths become unnecessary. He refers to the traditional understanding of not breaking oaths made to the Lord and extends it by advising against making oaths altogether. By cautioning against swearing by Heaven, Earth, Jerusalem, or one's own head, Jesus underscores that all creation belongs to God, and humans lack the authority to enlist divine creations as guarantors of their words. Instead, He urges His followers to speak plainly and truthfully at all times.

Key Points

1. **Integrity in Speech**
   Jesus encourages us to live a life where simple words are enough, reflecting inner truthfulness.
2. **Sanctity of Creation**
   By referencing Heaven, Earth, and Jerusalem, Jesus reminds us of the sacredness of creation and God's ultimate authority over it.

3. **Simplicity in Communication**
   Jesus advocates straightforward and honest communication, encouraging a simple 'Yes' or 'No' response.
4. **Avoidance of Manipulation**
   By prohibiting us from taking oaths, Jesus warns against manipulating others by using divine or significant elements to guarantee our words.
5. **The Root of Dishonesty**
   Jesus suggests that anything other than the truth comes from "the evil one," indicating that deception has no place in the life of a believer.

Exercises to Apply This Teaching

1. **Practice Plain Speaking**
   Make an effort to communicate clearly and directly, letting your 'Yes' be 'Yes,' and your 'No,' 'No.'
2. **Reflect on Your Words**
   At the end of each day, reflect on your conversations. Were there instances where you exaggerated, embellished, or were less than truthful? Understanding the reasons behind these moments can help you change this pattern.
3. **Commit to Truth**
   Make a personal commitment to speak truthfully in all situations, even when it's uncomfortable or it might not portray you in the best light.
4. **Understand the Weight of Words**
   Study or meditate on the power and impact of words, considering how they affect trust and relationships.
5. **Encourage Others to Integrity**
   When in conversations with others, encourage straightforward and honest dialogue.

Conclusion

In His teachings on oaths, Jesus is not merely reformulating legal practices but calling for a transformation in the way we communicate. He invites His followers to a higher standard of integrity and truthfulness that reflects the character of God. This teaching challenges us to examine the honesty of our speech and the purity of our intentions in all our communications.

Theologians' Take

Theologians frequently interpret this passage as Jesus' summons to sincere and honest communication, seeing it as part of a broader critique of the legalistic and ostentatious religiosity of the time. Some perceive it as a radical call to live in a manner where our words always reflect the truth, making oaths unnecessary. Others focus on the societal implications, considering how a community of truth-tellers could transform interactions and relationships. They propose that Jesus is pointing to the kingdom of God, where truth reigns and integrity is the norm, contrasting it with the fallen world where deceit comes naturally. The consensus is that Jesus elevates the disclosure of truth, emphasizing that it's not just about avoiding lies but about cultivating a character of transparency and reliability.

Chapter 10 – The Path of Non-Retaliation: Understanding 'Eye for Eye'

In Matthew 5:38-42, Jesus teaches us about retaliation. Here, Jesus addresses the Old Testament law of "an eye for an eye and a tooth for a tooth," a principle that was originally intended to limit retribution and ensure that punishment was proportional to the offense. However, Jesus suggests a radical new perspective.

"You have heard that it was said, 'Eye for eye, and tooth for tooth.' But I tell you, do not resist an evil person. If anyone slaps you on the right cheek, turn to them the other cheek also. And if anyone wants to sue you and take your shirt, hand over your coat as well. If anyone forces you to go one mile, go with them two miles. Give to the one who asks you, and do not turn away from the one who wants to borrow from you."

Understanding the Teaching

Jesus challenges the natural human instinct for revenge by advocating non-retaliation and even suggests generosity in the face of any wrongdoings. He encourages turning the other cheek, giving more than asked, and going the extra mile. This teaching isn't about passivity or tolerating injustice; it's about choosing a response that breaks the cycle of revenge and transforms potential conflict.

Key Points

1. **Reinterpreting Justice**
   Jesus reframes the concept of justice from retribution to restoration and reconciliation.

2. **Non-Retaliation**
   He encourages us not to retaliate against evil and suggests that true strength lies in maintaining integrity and showing love in the face of wrongdoing.
3. **Generosity in Response**
   Jesus encourages a generous and non-defensive posture, especially when faced with demands or aggression.
4. **Going Beyond**
   The theory behind going the extra mile indicates an active approach to love and service, exceeding what is required or expected from us.
5. **Empathy and Engagement**
   Offering the other cheek or giving more than asked for is about engaging with the offender in a way that can open doors to understanding and transformation.

Exercises to Apply This Teaching

1. **Practice Patience**
   Choose a response that seeks to de-escalate rather than retaliate. Suppose you feel wronged or provoked; take a deep breath and count to ten before responding.
2. **Active Generosity**
   Find an opportunity to be generous to someone who hasn't been kind or fair to you.
3. **Reflect on Provocations**
   Keep a journal of instances where you felt provoked or wronged, and reflect on how you responded versus how you could apply Jesus' teachings if they happen again.
4. **Go the Extra Mile**
   Voluntarily take on an extra task or help someone beyond what is expected of you, especially if it's someone with whom you've had differences.

5. Seek Understanding

In a conflict, make an effort to understand the other person's perspective and then respond in a way that acknowledges their humanity and dignity.

Conclusion

Jesus' teaching on "an eye for an eye" invites us to a higher standard of living, where acts of grace and forgiveness break the cycles of retribution. It's a call to live out the radical love and mercy that He exemplified, even in the face of injustice and offense.

Theologians' Take

Theologians often see this passage as a vivid illustration of Jesus' radical ethical teachings. They see it as a call to nonviolent resistance, not as submission to evil but as a powerful form of protest that refuses to perpetuate the cycle of violence. Some argue that it's about demonstrating the power of love and forgiveness to transform individuals and societies. Others view it as an impractical ideal, and some see it as a contextual teaching meant for specific situations rather than a blanket rule. Despite varied interpretations, many agree that this teaching challenges the natural human inclination toward revenge and invites a reconsideration of how justice and love intersect.

Chapter 11 – The Boundless Horizon of Love: Understanding 'Love Your Enemies'

In this chapter, we examine one of Jesus' most radical and transformative teachings found in Matthew 5:43-48. Jesus challenges the prevailing notion of loving one's neighbor and hating one's enemy. Instead, He commands His followers to love their enemies and pray for those who oppress them.

"You have heard that it was said, 'Love your neighbor and hate your enemy.' But I tell you, love your enemies and pray for those who persecute you, that you may be children of your Father in Heaven. He causes his sun to rise on the evil and the good, and sends rain on the righteous and the unrighteous. If you love those who love you, what reward will you get? Are not even the tax collectors doing that? And if you greet only your own people, what are you doing more than others? Do not even pagans do that? Be perfect, therefore, as your heavenly Father is perfect."

Understanding the Teaching

Jesus is not merely reforming an old law but revolutionizing the very concept of love itself. He broadens the command to love beyond family, tribe, and nation to encompass even those who are antagonistic. This love isn't rooted in feelings or emotions but is an act of the will—a choice to seek the good in others, regardless of their stance towards you.

Key Points

1. **Redefining Love**
   Jesus expands the definition of love to include everyone and not just those who are easy to love.

45

2. **Active Goodwill**
    Loving enemies involves active goodwill, doing good to those who may not do the same for you.
3. **Praying for Persecutors**
    Jesus specifically mentions a prayer for those who persecute you, indicating a desire for their well-being and transformation.
4. **Perfection as Aspiration**
    The call to be perfect as the heavenly Father is perfect as an aspiration to embody God's unconditional love and mercy.
5. **Breaking the Cycle of Hatred**
    This teaching is about breaking the cycle of hatred and animosity by inserting love where there is none.

Exercises to Apply This Teaching

1. **Pray for an Enemy**
    Regularly pray for someone who has wronged or hurt you, asking for their well-being and for your heart to be open to forgiveness.
2. **Acts of Kindness**
    Perform acts of kindness to those who either hold grudges against you or you have difficulties with them.
3. **Reflect on Love**
    Understand what it means to love unconditionally. How does it differentiate from the love you show others in your daily life?
4. **Seek Understanding**
    Try to understand the perspective of someone you consider an enemy or disagree with. Empathy should be the first step towards love.
5. **Meditate on God's Love**
    Meditate on how God loves humanity, including the flawed and the sinful. Consider how you might compete with that love in your own relationships.

Conclusion

Jesus' command to love your enemies is one of the most challenging and yet most liberating teachings. It calls us to rise above our instincts for retaliation and animosity and enter into a love that reflects the boundless nature of God's love for us. This teaching isn't just about changing how we treat others; it's about transforming our very understanding of love and expanding our capacity for it.

Theologians' Take

Theologians have wrestled with the implications of this command for a long time. Some view it as an ideal to strive towards, acknowledging the challenges but emphasizing its transformative potential. Others see it as a radical ethic that should reshape Christian interactions on personal, communal, and even international levels. There's also discussion about the notion of perfection in this passage, with many agreeing that it's about aspiring to the completeness and inclusivity of God's love rather than moral flawlessness. In short, theologians agree that this teaching calls for a profound reorientation of how love is understood and practiced.

Chapter 12 – The Grace of Giving: Understanding 'Give to the Needy'

In this chapter, we explore Jesus' teachings on charity and altruism found in Matthew 6:1-4. Jesus instructs His followers on the proper attitude and approach to giving to people in need, emphasizing the importance of sincerity and humility in acts of charity.

"Be careful not to practice your righteousness in front of others to be seen by them. If you do, you will have no reward from your Father in Heaven. So when you give to the needy, do not announce it with trumpets, as the hypocrites do in the synagogues and on the streets, to be honored by others. Truly I tell you, they have received their reward in full. But when you give to the needy, do not let your left hand know what your right hand is doing, so that your giving may be in secret. Then your Father, who sees what is done in secret, will reward you."

Understanding the Teaching

We learn that Jesus is against performing acts of charity for the sake of public recognition and admiration. Instead, He advocates to help and give in secret, ensuring that the act is between the giver and God only with no ulterior motives of self-glorification. This teaching isn't about discouraging generosity but about doing acts of kindness in secret so the other person doesn't feel belittled or incapable.

Key Points

1. **Sincerity in Charity**
   Charity is done out of real compassion and not for public approval.
2. **Rewards of the Righteous**
   While earthly praise is brief, the rewards from God for sincere charity are eternal and far more fulfilling.

3. **The Secret of Giving**
   Giving in secret preserves the dignity of the recipient and keeps the giver's intentions pure.
4. **Heart Over Showmanship**
   The emphasis is on the condition of the heart rather than the magnitude or visibility of the act.
5. **Divine Recognition**
   Acts done in secret are seen by God only, who is the ultimate judge and rewards our actions.

Exercises to Apply This Teaching

1. **Anonymous Giving**
   Make anonymous donations to a cause or an individual in need, ensuring that your act of giving is known only to you and God.
2. **Check Your Motives**
   Before giving, reflect on your motives. Are you seeking recognition, or are you genuinely moved to help?
3. **Offer Time**
   Beyond financial aid, give your time by volunteering for charitable organizations while keeping your service low-profile.
4. **Encourage Humble Giving**
   When discussing charity with friends or family, emphasize the importance of humility and sincerity rather than sharing specifics yourself.
5. **Pray for the Needy**
   Regularly include the less fortunate in your prayers, asking for not just their material provision but also their overall well-being.

Conclusion

Jesus' teaching on giving to the needy challenges us to examine the pureness of our intentions. It's a call to practice a form of generosity that is private, humble, and focused on the well-being of others, reflecting the selfless love of God. This approach to giving honors the recipient and aligns the giver with the righteousness that God desires.

Theologians' Take

Theologians often discuss this passage in the context of the broader Christian ethic of love and compassion. Many agree that Jesus is critiquing the religious hypocrisy of His day, where acts of charity were often done for show rather than out of genuine concern. The teaching is seen as a remedial, guiding believers to live out their faith authentically and without fanfare. Theologians also note the subversive nature of this teaching, as it challenges the societal norms of honor and recognition, proposing a form of giving that is radically private and personal.

Chapter 13 – The Heart of Conversation: Understanding Prayer

This chapter is all about Jesus' teachings on prayer, found in Matthew 6:5-15. Here, Jesus guides how to pray with sincerity, showing the difference between a hypocrite's prayer with that of the faithful.

"And when you pray, do not be like the hypocrites, for they love to pray standing in the synagogues and on the street corners to be seen by others. Truly I tell you, they have received their reward in full. But when you pray, go into your room, close the door and pray to your Father, who is unseen. Then your Father, who sees what is done in secret, will reward you. And when you pray, do not keep on babbling like pagans, for they think they will be heard because of their many words. Do not be like them, for your Father knows what you need before you ask him.

This, then, is how you should pray:

'Our Father in heaven,

hallowed be your name,

your kingdom come,

your will be done,

on Earth as it is in heaven.

Give us today our daily bread.

And forgive us our debts,

as we also have forgiven our debtors.

And lead us not into temptation,

but deliver us from the evil one.'

For if you forgive other people when they sin against you, your heavenly Father will also forgive you. But if you do not forgive others their sins, your Father will not forgive your sins."

Understanding the Teaching

Here, we learn that Jesus criticizes people who perform ostentatious prayers only to seek admiration from others. He instructs His followers to pray in private and focus on deep, personal communication with God. He then provides the Lord's Prayer as a model, which asks for God's will to be done, for daily bread, for forgiveness, and for protection against any temptation and evil.

Key Points

1. **Privacy in Prayer**
   A genuine prayer is a private communication between you and God and not a public performance.
2. **Simplicity in Words**
   A prayer from the heart is always simple and with much emotion that doesn't need any long description.
3. **The Lord's Prayer**
   This model prayer emphasizes God's kingdom, provision, forgiveness, and guidance.
4. **Forgiveness in Focus**
   One element of this prayer is the willingness to forgive others and, in turn, be forgiven by God.
5. **Guarding Against Temptation**
   You can also protect and resist temptations and any kind of evil through prayers.

Exercises to Apply This Teaching

1. **Private Prayer Time**
   Make a habit of praying daily. Isolate yourself away from distractions to better communicate with God.

2. **Pray the Lord's Prayer**
   Ingress the Lord's Prayer into your daily prayers to lead a better and fulfilling life.
3. **Journal Your Prayers**
   Keep a prayer journal to express your thoughts, requests, and reflections, helping to deepen your prayer life.
4. **Practice Forgiveness**
   Make a list of people you need to forgive and pray for the strength to forgive them, just as you seek God's forgiveness.
5. **Seek Guidance**
   Regularly ask for guidance in your prayers, specifically in areas where you're facing challenges or temptations.

Conclusion

Jesus' teachings on prayers enlighten us to a genuine, heartfelt conversation with God. Prayer is more than just about finding the right words; it is about saying right from the heart, like someone who seeks an intimate relationship with the Divine. This chapter encourages us to reflect on our prayer life and realign it with the principles Jesus taught, ensuring our prayers are not just heard but felt.

Theologians' Take

Theologians emphasize the revolutionary aspect of the Lord's Prayer in its communal language, diverging from the individualistic and earthly-focused prayers of the time. The instruction to pray privately challenges the idea of public piety as a measure of righteousness, redirecting attention to the individual's connection with God. The reciprocal nature of forgiveness in the prayer is also highlighted by theologians, reflecting a central theme in Jesus' teachings: receiving God's mercy is linked to extending mercy to others.

Chapter 14 – The Inner Sanctum of Sacrifice: Understanding Fasting

In Matthew 6:16-18, Jesus teaches about fasting. It is a practice of abstaining from food and other worldly pleasures. This is done as a spiritual exercise to deepen one's faith and reliance on God. Here, Jesus addresses the proper way with which to fast.

"When you fast, do not look somber as the hypocrites do, for they disfigure their faces to show others they are fasting. Truly I tell you, they have received their reward in full. But when you fast, put oil on your head and wash your face, so that it will not be obvious to others that you are fasting, but only to your Father, who is unseen; and your Father, who sees what is done in secret, will reward you."

Understanding the Teaching

This passage highlights the manner in which a believer fasts. Jesus emphasizes that a believer should fast in a way that honors God rather than seeking approval or recognition from others. He teaches His followers to fast in a way that is done in secrecy so only God knows. The emphasis is on the sincerity of the practice, not the external display.

Key Points

1. **Sincerity in Fasting**
   A proper fast is done in secret, with a heart oriented towards God and not for human approval.
2. **Inner Transformation**
   Fasting is an inward act of devotion and self-discipline that should lead to spiritual growth and deeper trust in God.
3. **Rewards of the Hidden**
   The rewards for sincere fasting are not public recognition but a closer, more intimate relationship with God.

4. **External Normalcy, Internal Focus**
   While fasting, individuals are to carry on with their regular appearance, keeping their focus inward and upward.
5. **Integrity in Practice**
   Fasting, like prayer and charity, is an exercise in integrity, aligning one's external actions with internal convictions.

Exercises to Apply This Teaching

1. **Try To Fast**
   Choose a day to fast from food, or if that's not advisable for health reasons, consider fasting from something else like social media or television.
2. **Journal Your Experience**
   During your fast, keep a journal and pen your thoughts, feelings, and any spiritual insights or struggles you face.
3. **Pray During Hunger Spasms**
   Whenever you feel hunger or a desire for the thing you're fasting from, use that as a prompt to pray or meditate.
4. **Break Your Fast Quietly**
   When your fast is over, break it quietly and without fanfare. Share the experience only if it brings encouragement or insight to others.
5. **Support a Cause**
   Consider donating the money or time you save from fasting to a charitable cause or someone in need

Conclusion

Jesus' teaching on fasting challenges us to examine why and how we engage in spiritual disciplines. It's not the act itself but the heart behind it that matters. This chapter encourages us to embrace fasting as a means to deepen our spiritual lives, strengthen our self-discipline, and enhance our connection with God, all the while maintaining an attitude of humility and sincerity.

Theologians' Take

Theologians view Jesus' teachings on fasting as part of a broader critique of religious hypocrisy. They note that Jesus does not condemn fasting itself but the pretentiousness that can accompany it. Many theologians see fasting as a practice that, when undertaken with the right intentions, can lead to profound spiritual growth and greater self-mastery. They also discuss the communal and ethical dimensions of fasting, suggesting that acts of charity and justice should accompany it.

Chapter 15 – The Eternal Investment: Understanding 'Treasures in Heaven'

This chapter is about Earthly and Heavenly treasures found in Matthew 6:19-24. Jesus contrasts the fleeting nature of material wealth with the enduring value of spiritual riches.

"Do not store up for yourselves treasures on Earth, where moths and vermin destroy, and where thieves break in and steal. But store up for yourselves treasures in heaven, where moths and vermin do not destroy, and where thieves do not break in and steal. For where your treasure is, there your heart will be also. The eye is the lamp of the body. If your eyes are healthy, your whole body will be full of light. But if your eyes are unhealthy, your whole body will be full of darkness. If then the light within you is darkness, how great is that darkness! No one can serve two masters. Either you will hate the one and love the other, or you will be devoted to the one and despise the other. You cannot serve both God and money."

Understanding the Teaching

Jesus advises against storing up treasures on Earth, where they are subject to decay and theft. Instead, He encourages focusing on storing treasures in heaven, where they are safe and secure.

He emphasizes that one's heart and treasures are intrinsically linked, suggesting that our priorities and values should be aligned with our spiritual goals. He concludes by saying that no one can serve two masters, highlighting the choice between God and material wealth.

Key Points

1. **Temporary vs. Eternal**
   Earthly treasures are temporary and vulnerable, while Heavenly treasures are permanent and secure.

2. **Heart's Alignment**
   Your heart will always be where your treasure is. This
   reveals our priorities and the affections we value.
3. **Better Health**
   The analogy of the lamp with the eye illustrates the
   importance of health. If our eyes are healthy, so are we and
   vice versa.
4. **Undivided Loyalty**
   The choice between serving God or wealth illustrates the
   impossibility of divided loyalties in the pursuit of spiritual
   enlightenment.
5. **Security and Peace**
   Investing in Heavenly treasures offers a sense of security and
   peace that Earthly wealth cannot provide.

Exercises to Apply This Teaching

1. **Inventory of Treasures**
   Reflect on what you consider your 'treasures.' How many are
   Earthly, and how many are spiritual? Consider how you can
   invest more in the latter.
2. **Act of Generosity**
   Choose to give away something you value one week,
   whether it's time, money, or a prized possession, to
   experience the joy of Heavenly investment.
3. **Daily Priorities Check**
   At the end of each day, evaluate where you spent most of
   your time and resources. Adjust as necessary to align more
   closely with spiritual priorities.
4. **Vision Check**
   Engage in a spiritual practice like meditation or prayer that
   helps clear your vision and focus on God's perspective.
5. **Community Focus**
   Invest in your community or church through volunteering,
   recognizing that relationships and service are key parts of
   storing up treasures in heaven.

Conclusion

This passage highlights the importance of focusing on spiritual treasures and maintaining a healthy spiritual perspective in life rather than being consumed by material wealth and worldly concerns.

This chapter encourages a reevaluation of priorities, urging a life focused on eternal values over temporary gains. It's an invitation to a life of purpose, generosity, and undivided devotion to God.

Theologians' Take

Theologians discuss this passage in the context of Christian ethics and eschatology. They note that Jesus is not condemning wealth per se but warning against the idolatry of wealth and the moral dangers of greed. Many emphasize the radical nature of Jesus' teachings on wealth, suggesting that they call for a profound reorientation of one's life and values. The passage is also seen as a comfort, offering a vision of God's kingdom where justice and peace prevail and where true riches are found in relationships, righteousness, and communion with God.

Chapter 16 – The Serenity of Surrender: Understanding 'Do Not Worry'

In this chapter, we explore Jesus' teachings on worry and anxiety as presented in Matthew 6:25-34. Here, Jesus tells His followers the importance of trusting in God and not to worry about material possessions.

"Therefore I tell you, do not worry about your life, what you will eat or drink; or about your body, what you will wear. Is not life more than food, and the body more than clothes? Look at the birds of the air; they do not sow or reap or store away in barns, and yet your Heavenly Father feeds them. Are you not much more valuable than they? Can any one of you by worrying add a single hour to your life?"

"And why do you worry about clothes? See how the flowers of the field grow. They do not labor or spin. Yet I tell you that not even Solomon in all his splendor was dressed like one of these. If that is how God clothes the grass of the field, which is here today and tomorrow is thrown into the fire, will He not much more clothe you—you of little faith? So do not worry, saying, 'What shall we eat?' or 'What shall we drink?' or 'What shall we wear?' For the pagans run after all these things, and your Heavenly Father knows that you need them. But seek first his kingdom and his righteousness, and all these things will be given to you as well. Therefore do not worry about tomorrow, for tomorrow will worry about itself. Each day has enough trouble of its own."

Understanding the Teaching

Jesus instructs His followers not to worry about life's basic needs as God will provide them. He uses the examples of birds and flowers, which are provided for by God, and how much more He can provide to His children. He encourages focusing on the kingdom of God and His righteousness, with the assurance that all these things will be added as well. The teaching concludes with the appeal to focus on the present and trust in God's provision for the future.

Key Points

1. **Value in God's Eyes**
   We are reminded of our worth to God, which far exceeds that of any of His creations.
2. **Provision of the Creator**
   Just as God provides for all His creatures, He will provide for us too.
3. **Priority of the Kingdom**
   Seeking God's kingdom and righteousness should be our primary concern, with the promise that our material needs will be met.
4. **Worrying is Futile**
   Jesus points out the pointlessness of worry. He says that each day has enough troubles of its own and that it is better to focus on the present and trust God in the future he has stored for us.

Exercises to Apply This Teaching

1. **Nature Meditation**
   Spend time with nature, observing God's creations and reflect how they are provided for while drawing parallels to your own life.

2. **Gratitude Journal**
   Keep a daily journal of things you're grateful for, including
   ways you've seen your needs met, which can help combat
   anxiety.
3. **Kingdom Focus**
   Engage in an activity that prioritizes the kingdom of God,
   such as volunteering, participating in community worship, or
   helping someone in need.
4. **Daily Concerns List**
   At the start of each day, write down your main concerns,
   then actively surrender each one to God in prayer.
5. **Limit Worry Time**
   Daily set aside a brief slot for worries, and if you get
   concerned about anything, write them down to revisit during
   your next 'worry period.'

Conclusion

Jesus' teaching on worry challenges us to reevaluate our focus and to
trust in God's provision and care. It's an invitation to release our
anxieties, understanding that our heavenly Father knows our needs
and is more than capable of meeting them. This chapter encourages
us to lead a life of faith, focusing on the present and pursuing God's
kingdom, promising peace and provision as we live in faith in God.

Theologians' Take

Theologians often view this passage as a profound commentary on
human anxiety and the nature of divine providence. Many agree that
Jesus is not advocating a careless or irresponsible attitude toward
life but promoting a radical trust in God that frees individuals from
the paralyzing effects of worry. They discuss the kingdom of God as
a present reality that provides a different set of values and priorities,
offering a perspective that transcends earthly concerns. The passage
is also seen as an invitation to a deeper spiritual life, where trust in
God leads to peace and contentment.

Chapter 17 – The Mirror of Judgment: Understanding 'Judging Others'

In Matthew 7:1-6, Jesus addresses the human tendency to judge others while often ignoring one's own faults.

"Do not judge, or you too will be judged. For in the same way you judge others, you will be judged, and with the measure you use, it will be measured to you. Why do you look at the speck of sawdust in your brother's eye and pay no attention to the plank in your own eye? How can you say to your brother, 'Let me take the speck out of your eye,' when all the time there is a plank in your own eye? You hypocrite, first take the plank out of your own eye, and then you will see clearly to remove the speck from your brother's eye. Do not give dogs what is sacred; do not throw your pearls to pigs. If you do, they may trample them under their feet, and turn and tear you to pieces."

Understanding the Teaching

Jesus begins with a straightforward command: "Do not judge, or you too will be judged." He warns that the way you judge others can be used against you, highlighting the reciprocal nature of judgment. Jesus then uses the metaphor of the speck and the plank, illustrating the folly of criticizing minor faults in others while being blind to one's own more significant issues.

He concludes with a caution about giving sacred things to those who will not appreciate them, implying the need for discernment in how and what we share about our faith.

Key Points

1. **Reciprocity in Judgment**
   The way we judge others will be the standard by which we are judged.
2. **Self-Reflection Over Criticism**
   Before judging others, we should reflect on our own lives and rectify our faults.
3. **Humility in Perception**
   Acknowledging our own imperfections leads to a more compassionate and understanding approach to others' faults.
4. **Discernment in Sharing**
   While not directly about judgment, the teaching about pearls and swine emphasizes the need for discernment in how we share the sacred aspects of our faith.
5. **Compassion and Correction**
   The call is not to abandon moral discernment but to approach it with humility, love, and an awareness of our own imperfection.

Exercises to Apply This Teaching

1. **Reflection Before Reaction**
   When you feel the urge to judge someone, take a moment to reflect on your own faults first. This can shift your perspective from judging to empathy.
2. **Act of Kindness**
   Do something kind for someone you've judged or criticized recently, changing your negative impression about them into a positive.
3. **Daily Self-Examination**
   At the end of each day, reflect on moments when you judged others. Consider what triggered those judgments and how you can respond differently in the future.

4. **Seek Understanding**
   When you find yourself judging someone, take a moment to observe and understand their situation. This might involve talking or simply contemplating possible reasons for their actions.
5. **Meditate on Mercy**
   Regularly meditate on the concept of mercy and how it's been applied to your life. Let this understanding guide how you view and interact with others.

Conclusion

Jesus' teaching on judging others challenges us to look inward before looking outward. It's a way to live with self-awareness, humility, and compassion, recognizing our own imperfections as we interact with others. This passage encourages us to replace judgment with understanding and criticism with kindness, reflecting the merciful nature of God in our lives.

Theologians' Take

Theologians discuss this passage in the context of Christian ethics and community life. Many have agreed that Jesus is not prohibiting moral discernment but, in fact, warning against a judgmental attitude that lacks love and self-awareness. The teaching is seen as a call to communal humility and mutual edification rather than condemnation. Theologians also note that the balance between holding to moral standards and offering grace emphasizes that righteous judgment must always be tempered with mercy and self-reflection.

Chapter 18 – The Door of Persistence: Understanding 'Ask, Seek, Knock'

In this chapter, we explore Jesus' teachings on persistence in prayer and seeking God's will, as presented in Matthew 7:7-12. Here, Jesus encourages His followers to continually ask, seek, and knock, assuring them that their persistence will be rewarded.

"Ask and it will be given to you; seek and you will find; knock and the door will be opened to you. For everyone who asks receives; the one who seeks finds; and to the one who knocks, the door will be opened. Which of you, if your son asks for bread, will give him a stone? Or if he asks for a fish, will give him a snake? If you then, though you are evil, know how to give good gifts to your children, how much more will your Father in Heaven give good gifts to those who ask him! So in everything, do to others what you would have them do to you, for this sums up the Law and the Prophets."

Understanding the Teaching

Jesus uses three verbs — ask, seek, and knock — to illustrate different aspects of prayer and the pursuit of God's kingdom. Ask indicates prayer and petition, seek suggests a deeper quest for understanding and relationship, and knock implies a request for entry or opportunity. He assures that those who engage in these actions will receive, find, and have doors opened to them. Jesus then emphasizes God's goodness and willingness to give good gifts to His children, much more than an Earthly father would. The teaching concludes with the golden rule, which encapsulates the Law and the Prophets: Treat others as you would want them to treat you.

Key Points

1. **Persistence in Prayer**
   Jesus encourages His followers to pray continuously and promises that they will be rewarded.
2. **God's Faithfulness**
   Jesus assures that God will respond to all the prayers, even if it takes time.
3. **Depth of Seeking**
   Seeking goes beyond superficial wants, digging into a deeper understanding and relationship with God.
4. **Opportunity and Openness**
   Knocking symbolizes the act of taking up opportunities and being open to what God provides.
5. **The Golden Rule**
   This principle summarizes the essence of Jesus' teachings on interpersonal relationships and is linked to the persistence in seeking God's will.

Exercises to Apply This Teaching

1. **Daily Asking**
   Set aside a fixed time each day to ask God for your needs, the needs of others, and the deeper desires of your heart.
2. **Active Seeking**
   Seek out activities that deepen your understanding of faith, such as Bible study, attending a lecture or discussion, or reading a spiritual book.
3. **Opportunity Knocking**
   Take a step towards an opportunity you've been hesitant about, whether it's a new service opportunity, a reconciliation effort, or a personal goal, and also pray about it.

4. **Reflect on God's Goodness**
   Reflect on times when God has answered your prayers or provided for you unexpectedly, and write them down as reminders of His benevolence.
5. **Live the Golden Rule**
   Each day, consciously do to others what you would want them to do to you, whether it's offering kindness, forgiveness, or help.

Conclusion

Jesus' teaching on asking, seeking, and knocking reassures us of God's responsiveness and invites us to a life of determined faith and action. It encourages an active, continuous engagement with God and a trust in His goodness and provision. This passage challenges us to not only ask with persistence but also to live out the principles of God's kingdom in our relationships with others.

Theologians' Take

Theologians discuss this passage in the context of the nature of prayer and God's responsiveness. Many highlight the relational aspect of prayer, seeing it as a dynamic interaction rather than a one-way request line. The teaching is also viewed as an encouragement for spiritual perseverance, suggesting that persistence in faith leads to spiritual growth and deeper understanding. Theologians link the golden rule to this persistence, noting that living out God's will naturally leads to treating others with love and respect.

Chapter 19 – The Path Less Traveled: Understanding 'The Narrow and Wide Gates'

Jesus teaches about the two paths of life found in Matthew 7:13-14. He presents a vivid image of two gates, one wide and one narrow, representing divergent paths with very different destinations.

"Enter through the narrow gate. For wide is the gate and broad is the road that leads to destruction, and many enter through it. But small is the gate and narrow the road that leads to life, and only a few find it."

Understanding the Teaching

Jesus warns against the wide gate and broad road, which many follow, leading to destruction. Instead, He insists His followers travel the narrow gate with the difficult path, which, though less traveled, leads to life. This metaphor is about the choices we make in life and their eternal implications.

Key Points

1. **Choice of Paths**
   Life presents two fundamental spiritual choices, each leading to a specific destination.
2. **Popularity vs. Truth**
   The wide path represents the easy, popular route, which contrasts with the truth and life found in the more challenging narrow path.
3. **Perseverance in Difficulty**
   The narrow path may be harder and less chosen, but it's the only way to true life and salvation.

4. **Discernment in Decision**
   Choosing the narrow path requires discernment, commitment, and often a countercultural stance.
5. **Eternal Implications**
   The choice of path has eternal consequences, underscoring the seriousness of our life decisions.

Exercises to Apply This Teaching

1. **Path Reflection**
   Reflect on areas of your life where you might be choosing the wide gate. Consider what it might look like if you choose the narrow gate instead.
2. **Check Decisions Daily**
   At the end of each day, review the decisions you've made. Was there any that you made to ease your life or did you choose the more difficult path to make other's life easy?
3. **Seek Guidance**
   Regularly pray for wisdom and guidance to discern and choose the narrow path in life's complex situations.
4. **Study the Lives of Saints**
   Read about individuals in history who chose the narrow path, reflecting on their challenges and triumphs as a source of inspiration.
5. **Community Support**
   Find or create a community of like-minded individuals who are also committed to walking the narrow path, offering support and accountability to each other.

Conclusion

Jesus' teaching about the narrow and wide gates compels us to consider which directions our lives should go including our penultimate destination. It's a call to deliberate, intentional living, choosing the path of truth, righteousness, and, sometimes, resistance over the easier, more popular routes. This chapter encourages a life of thoughtful discernment, courageous decision-making, and steadfast commitment to the journey toward eternal life.

Theologians' Take

Theologians discuss this passage in the context of Christian ethics and eschatology. Many see it as a stark reminder of the reality of judgment and the importance of living a life in line with God's will. The narrow gate is frequently interpreted as a metaphor for Jesus himself and the demanding nature of true discipleship. Theologians caution against using this passage to condemn others and instead emphasize its call to personal self-examination and commitment. The teaching is seen as both a comfort for those on the difficult path of righteousness and a sobering call to those who may be complacent.

Chapter 20 – Foundations of Life: Understanding 'The Wise and Foolish Builders'

The passage found in Matthew 7:24-27 explores Jesus' parable of the wise and foolish builders. This teaching concludes the Sermon on the Mount and emphasizes the importance of not only hearing Jesus' words but also acting upon them.

"Therefore everyone who hears these words of mine and puts them into practice is like a wise man who built his house on the rock. The rain came down, the streams rose, and the winds blew and beat against that house; yet it did not fall, because it had its foundation on the rock. But everyone who hears these words of mine and does not put them into practice is like a foolish man who built his house on the sand. The rain came down, the streams rose, and the winds blew and beat against that house, and it fell with a great crash."

Understanding the Teaching

Jesus compares those who hear and act on His teachings to a wise man who built his house on the rock. When the storm hit, the house stood firm. In comparison, those who hear but don't act are associated with a foolish man who built his house on the sand, and once the storm hits, his house is destroyed. This parable illustrates the foundational importance of living out Jesus' teachings in our lives.

Key Points

1. **Hearing and Doing**
   It's not enough to simply hear or intellectually agree with Jesus' teachings; we must also put them into practice.

2. **Foundation of Life**
   Our lives need a firm foundation, and Jesus' words provide that stability and security.
3. **Testing Through Trials**
   Life's inevitable storms test the strength of our foundation. Only a life built on Jesus' teachings will stand firm.
4. **The Illusion of Security**
   Appearances can be deceiving. Like houses that look the same externally, it's the unseen foundation that determines stability.
5. **Consequences of Choices**
   Our choices have real consequences, and choosing to ignore Jesus' words leads to ruin, much like the foolish builder's house.

Exercises to Apply This Teaching

1. **Reflect on Foundations**
   Reflect on what foundations your life is built upon. Are there areas where you're acting on sand rather than rock in a storm?
2. **Identify and Act**
   Identify one of Jesus' teachings that you struggle to put into practice. Create a plan to incorporate it into your daily life.
3. **Support System**
   Discuss with a friend or a small group how you can support each other in building your lives on the teachings of Jesus.
4. **Journaling the Storms**
   When you face trials, journal about them. Reflect on how your foundation in Christ is helping you withstand the storm.
5. **Study the Sermon on the Mount**
   Go back and study the entire Sermon on the Mount (Matthew 5-7), identifying key teachings to implement in your life.

Conclusion

The parable of the wise and foolish builders is a powerful illustration of the importance of living out the teachings of Jesus. It encourages us not to be complacent with just listening but to be active doers of these teachings in order to build our lives on a solid foundation. This passage challenges us to examine our lives and reinforce our foundations to ensure they can withstand life's storms.

Theologians' Take

Theologians often interpret this parable as a call to authentic discipleship, emphasizing the importance of obedience and the transformative power of putting faith into action. They discuss the nature of true wisdom as it relates to obedience and the deception of superficial faith. Many agree that this teaching is a culmination of the Sermon on the Mount, summarizing the radical, countercultural life to which Jesus calls His followers. The stark contrast between the two builders is seen as a reminder of the ultimate accountability and the eternal consequences of our choices.

Chapter 21 – Discerning the Authentic: Understanding 'True and False Prophets'

In this chapter, we examine Jesus' teachings about recognizing true and false prophets, as described in Matthew 7:15-20. Jesus warns us of false prophets who appear righteous but are inwardly deceitful and instructs us on how to recognize them.

"Watch out for false prophets. They come to you in sheep's clothing, but inwardly they are ferocious wolves. By their fruit you will recognize them. Do people pick grapes from thornbushes, or figs from thistles? Likewise, every good tree bears good fruit, but a bad tree bears bad fruit. A good tree cannot bear bad fruit, and a bad tree cannot bear good fruit. Every tree that does not bear good fruit is cut down and thrown into the fire. Thus, by their fruit you will recognize them."

Understanding the Teaching

Jesus describes the false prophets as wolves in sheep's clothing, signifying that they may appear harmless or even virtuous, but in truth, their intentions and actions are dangerous. He suggests that distinguishing between true and false prophets involves observing the outcomes and character of their teachings and actions, known as their fruits. This is further defined by saying that a good tree will produce good fruits, and a bad tree will produce bad fruits. In short, the true nature of a person is eventually revealed by their actions and the effects of their influence.

Key Points

1. **Deceptive Appearances**
   False prophets may seem benign or righteous, but their true nature is harmful.
2. **Fruit as Evidence**
   The true test of any prophet or teacher is the 'fruit' they produce — the quality and impact of their actions and teachings.
3. **Inherent Nature Revealed**
   Just as trees inevitably produce fruit according to their nature, people will ultimately reveal their true character.
4. **Need for Discernment**
   Discerning between true and false requires careful observation and judgment, not superficial assessment.
5. **Consequences of Following**
   Following a false prophet leads to destruction, just as a bad tree being eventually cut down and destroyed.

Exercises to Apply This Teaching

1. **Reflect on Influences**
   Reflect on the people who influence you spiritually. Look at how they live their own life and impact others as well.
2. **Cultivate Discernment**
   Regularly pray for wisdom and the ability to discern what is true and what is false.
3. **Study the Fruits**
   Study the fruits of the spirit as described in Galatians 5:22-23. Reflect on how these can be benchmarks to identify true prophets.
4. **Be a Fruit-Bearer**
   Focus on bearing good fruit in your own life. Choose one aspect, such as kindness or faithfulness, and consciously work on it.

5. **Community Discussion**
   Engage in discussions with your faith community about recent teachings or spiritual trends, analyzing them for their fruit based on biblical principles.

Conclusion

This passage serves as a caution to be discerning and not be misled by those who claim to be spiritual leaders but do not demonstrate goodness in their words and deeds. It reminds us that appearances can be deceiving and that the true test of any spiritual leader or movement is their character and the results of their influence. This passage encourages us to seek wisdom, cultivate discernment, and bear good fruit in our own lives as evidence of our authentic walk with God.

Theologians' Take

Theologians view this passage as an essential guideline for maintaining the purity and integrity of the Christian community. They discuss the nature of deception and the importance of doctrinal and ethical vigilance. Many emphasize the role of the Holy Spirit in providing discernment and the importance of a well-grounded biblical understanding to recognize falsehoods. The passage is also seen as a warning against the uncritical acceptance of charismatic or seemingly authoritative figures and a reminder that all leaders are accountable to God.

Chapter 22 – Essence Over Appearance: Understanding 'True and False Disciples'

In the passage of True and False Disciples from Matthew 7:21-23, Jesus differentiates between those who merely profess faith and those who genuinely live it.

"Not everyone who says to me, 'Lord, Lord,' will enter the kingdom of Heaven, but only the one who does the will of my Father who is in Heaven. Many will say to me on that day, 'Lord, Lord, did we not prophesy in your name and in your name drive out demons and in your name perform many miracles?' Then I will tell them plainly, 'I never knew you. Away from me, you evildoers!'"

Understanding the Teaching

Jesus asserts that simply calling Him 'Lord' and performing miraculous deeds is not enough to enter into the kingdom of Heaven. Instead, doing the will of His Father is what makes someone a true disciple. He warns of the day when many will claim their love for Him through their deeds, but He will declare that He doesn't know them because their actions were performed to gain favor and nothing else.

Key Points

1. **Obedience Over Lip Service**
   True discipleship is demonstrated through obedience to God's will and not just with a verbal profession of faith.
2. **The Danger of Self-Deception**
   It's possible to be self-deceived, thinking one is a disciple based on outward religious activities while lacking a true relationship with Christ.

3. **Intimacy with Jesus**
   There's a difference between knowing Jesus and being known by Him. It is about the personal, ongoing relationship and not just the spectacular deeds.

4. **Authenticity in Faith**
   Authentic discipleship involves sincerity and alignment between one's stated beliefs and actual practices.

5. **Judgment and Recognition**
   Jesus speaks of a future judgment where genuine disciples will be recognized, not by their achievements, but by their fidelity to God's will.

Exercises to Apply This Teaching

1. **Self-Reflection**
   Reflect on your relationship with Jesus. Do genuine intimacy and obedience characterize it, or are there areas of mere lip service?

2. **Obedience Check**
   Identify one aspect of God's will that you struggle with. Focus on aligning this area of your life more closely with His will through prayer and practical steps.

3. **Serve in Secret**
   Engage in a service or act of kindness without telling anyone or seeking recognition, focusing instead on the approval of God alone.

4. **Study the Word**
   Regularly study the Bible to understand God's will more deeply and apply it to your life, moving beyond superficial faith.

5. **Accountability Partnership**
   Form an accountability relationship with a fellow believer to encourage each other in pursuing authentic discipleship.

Conclusion

Jesus' teaching about true and false disciples is a powerful reminder that the essence of discipleship is found in a genuine relationship with Him, marked by obedience and intimacy.

It challenges us to examine the substance of our faith, moving beyond appearances and achievements to a heartfelt, committed walk with God. This passage encourages a life of authenticity, where our actions and faith are in harmony.

Theologians' Take

Theologians discuss this passage as a critical distinction between nominal Christianity and genuine faith. Many emphasize the importance of grace, noting that true discipleship is not about earning God's favor through deeds but responding to His grace with obedience. They caution against a performance-based faith that focuses on external achievements rather than internal transformation. This teaching is also seen as a warning against spiritual complacency and a call to continual self-examination and growth in the Christian journey.

Chapter 23 – The Conclusion of the Sermon on the Mount

As we conclude this pivotal section of Matthew's Gospel, we reflect on the profound and revolutionary teachings Jesus delivered. His words, marked by authority and depth, left the crowds amazed and continue to inspire readers today.

The Sermon's Conclusion (Matthew 7:28-29)

"When Jesus had finished saying these things, the crowds were amazed at his teaching, because he taught as one who had authority, and not as their teachers of the law."

Key Points of the Sermon on the Mount

1. **The Beatitudes (Matthew 5:3-12)**
   Jesus begins with blessings for the poor in spirit, the mournful, the meek, and others who, in their humility and longing for righteousness, find the kingdom of Heaven.
2. **Salt and Light (Matthew 5:13-16)**
   Followers of Jesus are called to influence the world positively, preserving goodness and illuminating truth.
3. **Fulfillment of the Law (Matthew 5:17-20)**
   Jesus emphasizes that He came not to abolish the Law but to fulfill it, calling for a righteousness that surpasses that of the Pharisees.
4. **Teachings on Anger, Lust, Divorce, and Oaths (Matthew 5:21-37)**
   He intensifies the understanding of the Law, focusing on the heart's intent rather than just external compliance.
5. **Love for Enemies (Matthew 5:43-48)**
   Jesus commands to love not only your neighbors but also your enemies – reflecting the perfect love of the Father.

6. **Giving to the Needy, Prayer, and Fasting (Matthew 6:1-18)**
   These acts of devotion should be done sincerely and not for public acceptance.
7. **Treasures in Heaven (Matthew 6:19-24)**
   True security is found in heavenly treasures, not earthly.
8. **Do Not Worry (Matthew 6:25-34)**
   Jesus encourages trust in God's provision, urging focus on the kingdom over anxious thoughts about daily needs.
9. **Judging Others (Matthew 7:1-6)**
   He warns against hypocrisy in judgment, advising to first address one's own faults.
10. **Ask, Seek, Knock (Matthew 7:7-12)**
    Resolve in prayer is encouraged, along with the assurance of God's good gifts.
11. **The Narrow and Wide Gates (Matthew 7:13-14)**
    A call to choose the challenging yet rewarding path of true discipleship.
12. **True and False Prophets (Matthew 7:15-20)**
    Good judgment is needed to recognize true teachers by their fruits.
13. **True and False Disciples (Matthew 7:21-23)**
    Not all who profess faith will enter the kingdom, but those who perform God's will.
14. **The Wise and Foolish Builders (Matthew 7:24-27)**
    The parable concludes the sermon, emphasizing the importance of not only hearing Jesus' words but acting on them.

Theologians' Take on The Sermon on The Mount

Theologians regard The Sermon on The Mount as one of the most significant and challenging pieces of ethical teachings in human history. Many view it as the essence of Christian moral life, offering a radical alternative to the world's values. The sermon is seen as both a comfort for the oppressed, promising them the kingdom of

Heaven, and a challenge to the complacent, urging a deeper, more authentic commitment to living out God's will.

❖ **Radical Ethic**
Theologians note the sermon's radical nature, pushing listeners to strengthen their faith and belief in God and His teachings.

❖ **Kingdom-Oriented Life**
The teachings are often viewed as depicting life in God's kingdom, characterized by mercy, purity, peace-making, and righteousness.

❖ **Realistic Idealism**
While some argue that the sermon sets an unattainably high standard, others suggest that it provides an ideal for Christians to strive toward as laid out by Jesus.

❖ **Social Implications**
Many theologians discuss the sermon's implications for social justice, non-violence, and community living, suggesting that it calls for a transformative way of life that impacts every aspect of society.

As we move forward, we'll discuss and dissect Jesus' other teachings, metaphors, and riddles in order to explore the depth and breadth of His instructions for a life aligned with the kingdom of God.

Part two

As we turn the page from the rich tapestry of principles and actions that define a faithful leader, we find ourselves at a pivotal juncture. Part 1 has laid the groundwork, instilling in us the virtues of humility, compassion, and integrity. With these guiding lights, we now venture forth, much like a traveler who has prepared diligently for a journey of great consequence.

In Part 2, we follow in the footsteps of one of history's most quintessential leaders: Jesus of Nazareth. The Sermon on the Mount has concluded, leaving the echoes of its profound lessons to resonate in the hearts of those who heard it. Jesus now descends from the mount, his feet set upon the dusty roads that weave through towns and villages, his heart open to the multitudes that seek His wisdom and His healing touch.

This transition is not just a change of setting, but a profound shift in the ministry of Jesus. He moves from preaching to practicing; teaching to touching lives directly. It is here, among the people, that his teachings take on flesh and blood, as he extends his mercies and deepens his engagement with the troubled souls of the world. This is not a mission to conquer lands or amass followers but a calling to save souls, one by one, with acts of love and miracles of faith.

As leaders in our own journeys, we are called to emulate this transition. To step down from our places of contemplation and planning, and to walk amongst those we lead. To expand our reach not by power or decree, but through the compassionate and humble sharing of our teachings and the offering of our service. To remember, as Jesus demonstrates, that true leadership is found not in the throngs of the world's acclaim, but in the quiet places where one soul can reach another.

Let us then proceed, with the lessons of Chapter 2 etched into our characters, ready to walk the paths of our respective missions, broadening our teachings, and deepening our mercies, in the sacred pursuit of guiding souls towards the light.

This transition not only reflects the change in narrative direction but also draws a parallel between the leadership principles discussed and the example set by Jesus as he begins his work among the people, aligning the reader's journey with the broader themes of service and humility.

Chapter 24 – Compassion in Action: Understanding Jesus' Healing of the Leper

In this chapter, we explore the account of Jesus healing a man with leprosy as recounted in Matthew 8:1-4. This event occurs just after Jesus descends from the mount, illustrating His teachings through a powerful act of healing and compassion.

"When Jesus came down from the mountainside, large crowds followed him. A man with leprosy came and knelt before him and said, 'Lord, if you are willing, you can make me clean.' Jesus reached out his hand and touched the man. 'I am willing,' he said. 'Be clean!' Immediately he was cleansed of his leprosy. Then Jesus said to him, 'See that you don't tell anyone. But go, show yourself to the priest and offer the gift Moses commanded, as a testimony to them.'"

Understanding the Teaching

The story portrays a man with leprosy, a condition that made him an outcast in society. He approached Jesus with nothing but his faith and humility so he could ask to be healed. Jesus, moved by compassion, touches the man with his hand and heals him, an act that breaks significant social and religious taboos. Jesus then instructs the man to follow the Law by visiting the priest and making an offering. This reinforced his respect for the Law and provided a testimony to the priests.

Key Points

1. **Faith and Humility**
   The man approached Jesus with faith in His ability to heal demonstrating Jesus' authority and divine nature.
2. **Compassion Over Convention**
   Jesus' willingness to touch the leper demonstrates His prioritization of compassion over societal norms and legal restrictions regarding uncleanness.
3. **Instantaneous Healing**
   The immediate response to Jesus' command underscores His divine authority and power.
4. **Adherence to the Law**
   Jesus respects the Law of Moses. Hence, He instructs the healed man to present himself to the priest and make an offering.
5. **Discretion and Testimony**
   Jesus advises the man not to publicize the miracle but to offer a testimony to the religious leaders, possibly to challenge their understanding of the Messiah.

Exercises to Apply This Teaching

1. **Reach Out in Compassion**
   Identify someone in your community who is marginalized or suffering. Find a way to provide support, breaking out of your comfort zone if necessary.
2. **Faith Reflection**
   Reflect on areas of your life where you need healing or help. Approach God with the same faith and humility shown by the leper.
3. **Study and Respect**
   Learn more about the laws and customs of Jesus' time to understand His actions and teachings better. Reflect on how respect for Law and tradition can coexist with the need for reform and compassion.

4. **Share Your Testimony**
   If you've experienced healing or transformation in your life, share them as a testament to your faith so that the believers can further strengthen their faith as well.
5. **Prayer for the Marginalized**
   Regularly pray for those who are marginalized in society, asking for guidance on how you can be an agent of compassion and change.

Conclusion

The healing of the leper is a powerful demonstration of Jesus' authority, compassion, and willingness to challenge societal norms for the sake of love. It challenges us to examine how we can reflect Jesus' compassion in our own lives, reaching out to those in need, acting with humility and faith, and living in a way that provides a powerful testimony to the transformative power of God's love.

Theologians' Take

Theologians discuss this miracle in the context of Jesus' role as a healer and a social reformer. They note that by touching the leper, Jesus not only cleanses him physically but also begins to dismantle the barriers of impurity and exclusion that marginalized many in society. This act is seen as a radical challenge to the religious and social norms of the day, reflecting the inclusivity and compassion at the heart of Jesus' ministry. The instruction to not publicize the miracle but to show himself to the priest is often interpreted as a strategic move to provoke thought and recognition among the religious leaders about Jesus' identity and authority.

Chapter 25 – The Power of Unseen Faith: Understanding 'The Faith of the Centurion'

In the passage, The Faith of the Centurion from Matthew 8:5-13, we learn that this event is not only a testament to the power of faith but also a significant interaction between Jesus and a Roman Centurion, a representative of the occupying force in Israel at the time.

"When Jesus had entered Capernaum, a centurion came to him, asking for help. 'Lord,' he said, 'my servant lies at home paralyzed, suffering terribly.' Jesus said to him, 'Shall I come and heal him?' The centurion replied, 'Lord, I do not deserve to have you come under my roof. But just say the word, and my servant will be healed. For I myself am a man under authority, with soldiers under me. I tell this one, 'Go,' and he goes; and that one, 'Come,' and he comes. I say to my servant, 'Do this,' and he does it.' When Jesus heard this, he was amazed and said to those following him, 'Truly I tell you, I have not found anyone in Israel with such great faith. I say to you that many will come from the East and the West, and will take their places at the feast with Abraham, Isaac and Jacob in the kingdom of Heaven. But the subjects of the kingdom will be thrown outside, into the darkness, where there will be weeping and gnashing of teeth.' Then Jesus said to the centurion, 'Go! Let it be done just as you believed it would.' And his servant was healed at that moment."

Understanding the Teaching

A Centurion was a professional officer in the Roman army, commanding roughly 80-100 soldiers. They were known for their discipline, loyalty, and authority. The Centurion in this story approaches Jesus, pleading for the healing of his paralyzed servant. Despite his authority and status, he exhibits remarkable humility and faith, acknowledging Jesus' authority and expressing the belief that

Jesus can heal with just a word. Jesus marvels at this Gentile's faith, declaring it greater than any He had found in Israel, and the servant is healed at that very moment.

Key Points

1. **Authority Recognized**
   The Centurion recognizes Jesus' spiritual authority, likening it to his own command over soldiers.
2. **Faith Without Borders**
   The Centurion, a Gentile, demonstrates a faith that impresses Jesus, breaking cultural and religious barriers.
3. **Humility in Power**
   Despite his status, the centurion approaches Jesus with humility, understanding the true source of healing power.
4. **Healing at a Distance**
   Jesus' ability to heal the servant from afar showcases His divine authority and the power of faith.
5. **Inclusivity of the Kingdom**
   Jesus' commendation of the centurion's faith hints at the inclusive nature of the Kingdom of God, which is open to all who believe.

Exercises to Apply This Teaching

1. **Authority Reflection**
   Reflect on the areas where you have authority or influence. Consider how you can use this to impact others and honor God positively.

2. **Prayer of Faith**
   Pray for someone in need, believing in Jesus' power to heal and work in their life, even if the situation seems distant or difficult.

3. **Cultural Bridge-Building**
   Engage with someone from a different cultural or religious background. Learn from them, and share your own faith humbly and respectfully.
4. **Recognize Humility**
   Identify a situation where you need to approach it with more humility. Pray for the grace to do so and take a step in that direction.
5. **Study Inclusivity**
   Study other biblical instances where Jesus interacts with Gentiles or those outside the Jewish faith, reflecting on the inclusive nature of His ministry.

Conclusion

The faith of the centurion is a powerful testament to the significance of faith, humility, and understanding authority. It shows that true faith knows no boundaries and that Jesus' healing and salvation are available to all who believe, regardless of their background or status. This story challenges us to examine the depth of our faith and the humility with which we approach God and others.

Theologians' Take

Theologians point to this story as an illustration of the universal scope of Jesus' mission. The centurion is a symbol of Roman authority, and Gentile receives commendation for his faith, highlighting that faith is not confined to specific people or nations. Theologians also discuss the nature of faith and authority, noting how the centurion's understanding of Jesus' authority over sickness mirrors our call to recognize and trust in Jesus' spiritual authority over our lives. The story is seen as a challenge to preconceived notions of worthiness and an invitation to a faith that transcends cultural and religious barriers.

Chapter 26 – The Price and Privilege: Understanding 'The Cost of Following Jesus'

This chapter is about the cost of discipleship found in Matthew 8:18-22. This passage provides a stark look at the sacrifices required to follow Jesus, underscoring the depth of commitment needed.

"When Jesus saw the crowd around him, he gave orders to cross to the other side of the lake. Then a teacher of the law came to him and said, 'Teacher, I will follow you wherever you go.' Jesus replied, 'Foxes have dens and birds have nests, but the Son of Man has no place to lay his head.' Another disciple said to him, 'Lord, first let me go and bury my father.' But Jesus told him, 'Follow me, and let the dead bury their own dead.'"

Understanding the Teaching

As Jesus prepares to cross the lake, a teacher of the law approaches Him, promising to follow wherever He goes. Jesus responds by highlighting the lack of security and comfort in following Him, comparing His own itinerant lifestyle to the foxes and birds that have more stable homes. Another disciple asks to first go and bury his father, a request Jesus challenges, urging immediate and total commitment. This teaching confronts potential followers with the reality that discipleship requires sacrificing even the closest thing that matters to you.

Key Points

1. **Lack of Earthly Security**
   Following Jesus might mean giving up physical comforts and security, as true discipleship focuses on spiritual rather than material stability.
2. **Immediate Commitment**
   Jesus emphasizes the urgency and priority of following Him, superseding any personal and social duties.
3. **Understanding the Cost**
   Potential followers are encouraged to count the cost and understand the sacrifices involved in true discipleship.
4. **Unconditional Allegiance**
   The call to follow Jesus demands an allegiance that surpasses all other ties and commitments.
5. **Rewards of Discipleship**
   While not explicitly mentioned in this passage, other teachings of Jesus assure that while the cost is high, the eternal rewards and fulfillment far outweigh it.

Exercises to Apply This Teaching

1. **Personal Inventory**
   Reflect on what comforts or securities might be holding you back from fully committing to follow Jesus.
2. **Priority Check**
   For one week, consciously prioritize your spiritual commitments over personal or social obligations. Reflect daily on the impact of these choices.
3. **Study Discipleship**
   Study the lives of the disciples and other historical figures who have given up much to follow Jesus. Note the challenges they faced and the impacts they made.

4. **Cost and Reward Reflection**
   Write down the 'costs' of following Jesus you've experienced or might face. Then, write down the rewards and benefits you believe come with being His disciple. Reflect on the balance.
5. **Community Discussion**
   Engage in a discussion with your faith community about what the cost of discipleship looks like in your specific context. Encourage each other to live out this commitment.

Conclusion

This passage emphasizes the level of difficulties and commitment of following Jesus and His teachings to become a devoted disciple. With this, we understand what is required from us as faithful followers and what we should give up to remain firm with our resolve. This passage doesn't just outline the sacrifices but invites us to a deeper understanding and appreciation of the privilege of following Christ, despite the heavy costs.

Theologians' Take

Theologians discuss this passage as a critical moment of teaching about the radical nature of discipleship. They emphasize that Jesus isn't just seeking followers; He's calling for committed disciples whose allegiance to Him surpasses everything else. Theologians also reflect on the paradox of discipleship — that in giving up our lives, we find true life in Christ. They consider the implications of this teaching for the contemporary church, questioning how modern forms of Christianity align with the sacrificial call presented by Jesus.

Chapter 27 – The Master of the Seas: Understanding 'Jesus Calms the Storm'

This chapter revisits the event where Jesus calms the storm, as mentioned in Matthew 8:23-27. This dramatic scene not only demonstrates Jesus' power over nature but also highlights His ability to bring peace in the midst of any storm.

"Then he got into the boat and his disciples followed him. Suddenly a furious storm arises up on the lake, so that the waves swept over the boat. But Jesus was sleeping. The disciples went and woke him, saying, 'Lord, save us! We're going to drown!'"

"He replied, 'You of little faith, why are you so afraid?' Then he got up and rebuked the winds and the waves, and it was completely calm."

"The men were amazed and asked, 'What kind of man is this? Even the winds and the waves obey him!'"

Understanding the Teaching

As Jesus and His disciples cross the lake, a furious storm arises, threatening to overturn the boat. The disciples, fearing for their lives, wake Jesus, who is asleep. They plead to Him for His protection as they think they will drown. Jesus then calms the wind and the waves, and suddenly, the whole sea is quiet. But before that, He comments on the faith of His disciples, letting them know that having a strong faith in challenging times is essential. The disciples are left in awe, marveling at the authority of one whom even the wind and waves obey.

Key Points

1. **Divine Authority**
   Jesus demonstrates His authority over nature, a power that only God possesses, reinforcing His divine identity.
2. **Faith vs. Fear**
   The disciples' fear contrasts with the faith Jesus expects. This event challenges them (and us) to trust in Jesus' power and presence.
3. **Peace in Peril**
   Jesus can bring peace and calm to the most tumultuous situations, a metaphor for His ability to soothe our personal and spiritual storms.
4. **Awakening to Jesus**
   The disciples had to wake Jesus up, a reminder that we often need to turn to Him actively and seek His intervention in our crises.
5. **Marvel at His Majesty**
   The disciples' awe reflects the proper response to Jesus' divine power and authority.

Exercises to Apply This Teaching

1. **Storm Reflection**
   Reflect on a storm in your life, whether past or present. Write down how you responded or are responding. Are you turning to Jesus and trusting in His power?
2. **Faith Building**
   Identify areas of your life where your faith is weak. Engage in spiritual practices like prayer, scripture reading, or speaking with a mentor to build your faith.
3. **Peace Practice**
   When you feel anxious or afraid, practice calming your mind through prayer, meditation, or deep breathing, focusing on Jesus' presence and power.

4. **Nature Meditation**
    Spend time in nature, observing the elements — wind, water, earth. Reflect on Jesus' authority over all these and find comfort in His control over the universe.
5. **Share Your Story**
    Share the story of a personal 'storm' and how your faith helped you through it with someone who might be struggling so they can be encouraged.

Conclusion

The account of Jesus calming the storm is a powerful illustration of His divine authority and His ability to bring peace into our lives, no matter how chaotic or threatening the situation is. It calls us to a deeper faith, to trust in Him not only as the teacher and healer but as the Lord over all creation. This passage encourages us to turn to Jesus in our moments of fear and to stand in awe of His mighty power and loving presence.

Theologians' Take

Theologians view this story as a profound statement about Jesus' identity, noting that control over the natural world is a divine prerogative. They discuss the significance of the disciples' fear and lack of understanding, seeing it as reflective of the human condition — quick to fear and slow to faith. The calming of the storm is also seen symbolically, representing Jesus' power to bring peace to the chaos in the human heart and the world. Theologians emphasize that this miracle, like others, points to the deeper truth of Jesus' mission to save and restore.

Chapter 28 – The Authority of a Single Word: Understanding 'Jesus Heals the Demon-Possessed'

This passage of Matthew 8:28-34 tells us about how Jesus healed 2 men possessed by demons. This event showcases Jesus' supreme authority over the spiritual realm with just a single command: "Go."

"When he arrived at the other side in the region of the Gadarenes, two demon-possessed men coming from the tombs met him. They were so violent that no one could pass that way. 'What do you want with us, Son of God?' they shouted. 'Have you come here to torture us before the appointed time?'"

"Some distance from them a large herd of pigs was feeding. The demons begged Jesus, 'If you drive us out, send us into the herd of pigs.'"

"He said to them, 'Go!' So they came out and went into the pigs, and the whole herd rushed down the steep bank into the lake and died in the water. Those tending the pigs ran off, went into the town and reported all this, including what had happened to the demon-possessed men. Then the whole town went out to meet Jesus. And when they saw him, they pleaded with him to leave their region."

Understanding the Teaching

Jesus encounters two men possessed by demons who are so violent that no one can pass by them. The demons recognize Jesus as the Son of God and, knowing their impending doom, beg Him to send them into a herd of pigs instead. With one word, "Go," Jesus exorcises the demons, and they enter the pigs, who then run down the steep bank into the lake and die. This miracle demonstrates

Jesus' authority over evil forces and His power to restore those bound by them.

Key Points

1. **Recognition of Authority**
   Even the demons recognize Jesus' divine authority, addressing Him as the Son of God.
2. **Power in a Word**
   Jesus requires only a single word to cast out the demons, highlighting His supreme command over spiritual forces.
3. **Restoration and Impact**
   The healing of the demon-possessed men shows Jesus' power to restore individuals to their right mind and spirit.
4. **Response to the Miracle**
   The townspeople, unable to comprehend the miracle, become afraid and request Jesus to leave.
5. **Conflict of Kingdoms**
   The event illustrates the ongoing conflict between the kingdom of God and the forces of evil.

Exercises to Apply This Teaching

1. **Authority Acknowledgment**
   Reflect on areas of your life requiring Jesus' authority and intervention. Pray, inviting Him to work powerfully in these situations.
2. **Word of God Focus**
   Choose a verse or passage from the Bible that speaks to an area where you need freedom or healing. Meditate on it daily, believing in the power of God's word.
3. **Community Restoration**
   Engage in an activity that promotes healing and restoration in your community, whether through volunteering, prayer groups, or support networks.

4. **Reflect on Responses**
   Reflect on how you respond to the miraculous or challenging teachings of Jesus. Are you open, fearful, dismissive? Consider why and how you might cultivate a more receptive heart.
5. **Study Spiritual Warfare**
   Spend time studying the biblical perspective on spiritual warfare. Understand your position and authority in Christ over spiritual darkness.

Conclusion

The healing of the demon-possessed men in the Gadarenes region is a powerful testament to Jesus' authority over the forces of darkness. With just one word, He frees the men from the torment they are in. This story challenges us to recognize the spiritual battles around us and the authority Jesus has when confronting them. It's a call to rely on His power to bring liberation and peace into our lives and the lives of others.

Theologians' Take

Theologians discuss this event in the context of Christ's cosmic battle against evil. They note that Jesus' authority over demons is a sign of the inbreaking of God's kingdom, where the forces that bind and degrade humanity are defeated. The reaction of the townspeople is also of interest, as it highlights the various ways people respond to Jesus' power and presence. Theologians remind us that Jesus' mission was not just about physical healing but about a deeper spiritual restoration and reconciliation between God and humanity.

Chapter 29 – The Authority to Forgive: Understanding 'Jesus Forgives and Heals a Paralyzed Man'

In this section of the chapter, we are told how Jesus is forgiving and heals a paralyzed man (Matthew 9:2-8). This event not only demonstrates Jesus' power to heal but, more profoundly, His authority to forgive sins.

"Some men brought to him a paralyzed man, lying on a mat. When Jesus saw their faith, he said to the man, 'Take heart, son; your sins are forgiven.' At this, some of the teachers of the law said to themselves, 'This fellow is blaspheming!' Knowing their thoughts, Jesus said, 'Why do you entertain evil thoughts in your hearts? Which is easier: to say, 'Your sins are forgiven,' or to say, 'Get up and walk'? But I want you to know that the Son of Man has authority on Earth to forgive sins.' So he said to the paralyzed man, 'Get up, take your mat and go home.' Then the man got up and went home. When the crowd saw this, they were filled with awe; and they praised God, who had given such authority to man."

Understanding the Teaching

Some random people bring a paralyzed man to Jesus for healing. Seeing their faith, He first addresses the man's sins, announcing that the man is now absolved of them. This statement astonishes the onlookers and draws criticism from some scribes, who consider it blasphemy, as only God can forgive sins. Jesus, already aware of their thoughts, challenges them by asking which is easier to say, 'Your sins are forgiven,' or 'Get up and walk?'

To prove His authority to forgive sins, He then heals the man, commanding him to rise, take up his bed, and go home, which the man does promptly.

Key Points

1. **Forgiveness Precedes Healing** \
   Jesus first forgives the man's sins, indicating that spiritual healing is paramount.
2. **Authority of Jesus**
   The incident highlights Jesus' divine authority to forgive sins, a prerogative thought to belong to God alone.
3. **Faith's Role**
   The faith of the paralyzed man and his friends is central to the story, showing that faith is crucial in seeking Jesus' intervention.
4. **Challenge to Skepticism**
   Jesus addresses the skeptics directly, demonstrating His power and affirming His identity.
5. **Physical and Spiritual Restoration**
   The healing serves as a visible sign of the man's spiritual forgiveness and Jesus' authority in both realms.

Exercises to Apply This Teaching

1. **Reflect on Forgiveness**
   Reflect on areas in your life where you need Jesus' forgiveness. Pray for spiritual healing and restoration.
2. **Faith in Action**
   Like the friends of the paralyzed man, take a step of faith on behalf of someone else. It could be bringing their needs to Jesus in prayer or practically helping them in any way possible.
3. **Confront Skepticism**
   Reflect on any skepticism you might have about Jesus' teachings and miracles. Consider what evidence or assurance you need and seek those answers through study and prayer.

4. **Offer Forgiveness**
   If there's someone you need to forgive, take steps toward forgiveness, remembering the grace you've received from Jesus.
5. **Share Your Story**
   If you've experienced healing or forgiveness, share your story with someone as an encouragement and a testament to Jesus' power.

Conclusion

The event of healing the paralyzed man strongly illustrates Jesus' dual authority to forgive sins and heal physical ailments. It challenges us to recognize and embrace Jesus' divine identity and to understand the deep connection between spiritual forgiveness and physical restoration. This passage encourages us to seek Jesus for both, with faith in His power and authority.

Theologians' Take

Theologians discuss this passage in the context of Christ's messianic identity and divine authority. They note that forgiveness of sins is a central theme in Jesus' ministry and a primary aspect of the salvation He offers. The miracle serves as a sign of the inbreaking kingdom of God, where healing and forgiveness flow from Jesus' words and actions. Theologians also reflect on the role of faith and community in seeking Jesus' intervention, as seen in the actions of the paralyzed man's friends.

Chapter 30 – The Physician for the Soul: Understanding 'It is not the healthy who need a doctor, but the sick'

Here, we explore Jesus' statement in Matthew 9:10-13, a response to the Pharisees' criticism of Him eating with tax collectors and sinners. This teaching is a cornerstone of Jesus' ministry, emphasizing His mission to heal and restore those who recognize their spiritual need.

"While Jesus was having dinner at Matthew's house, many tax collectors and sinners came and ate with him and his disciples. When the Pharisees saw this, they asked his disciples, 'Why does your teacher eat with tax collectors and sinners?' On hearing this, Jesus said, 'It is not the healthy who need a doctor, but the sick. But go and learn what this means: 'I desire mercy, not sacrifice.' For I have not come to call the righteous, but sinners.'"

Understanding the Teaching

When Jesus says, "It is not the healthy who need a doctor, but the sick," He is responding to the Pharisees who questioned why He would associate with those deemed sinners. Jesus uses the analogy of a physician treating the ill to explain His focus on those spiritually lost or in need. He is highlighting that His mission is not to call the righteous (or those who perceive themselves as such) but sinners to repent.

Key Points

1. **Spiritual Sickness**
   Jesus acknowledges the spiritual sickness that plagues humanity, an ailment that He has come to heal.
2. **Inclusivity of Jesus' Mission**
   Jesus' willingness to dine with tax collectors and sinners illustrates His inclusive approach, extending grace to all, regardless of their social standing or past.
3. **Recognition of Need**
   The first step to receiving Jesus' healing is acknowledging one's own spiritual sickness and need for a physician.
4. **Contrast with Self-Righteousness**
   Jesus implicitly criticizes the Pharisees' self-righteousness, which blinds them to their need for spiritual healing.
5. **Repentance and Restoration**
   The purpose of Jesus' association with sinners is not to condone sin but to lead to repentance and restoration.

Exercises to Apply This Teaching

1. **Self-Examination**
   Reflect on your spiritual health. Are there areas of sin or sickness you need to bring to Jesus in order to get His help?
2. **Inclusive Community**
   Make an effort to extend your friendship and kindness to those who might feel excluded or marginalized in your community, reflecting Jesus' inclusive love.
3. **Study on Grace**
   Spend time studying other biblical stories and teachings about grace, repentance, and restoration. Reflect on how they apply to your life.
4. **Prayer for Healing**
   Regularly pray for spiritual healing for yourself and others, asking Jesus to reveal and heal areas of spiritual sickness.

5. **Share Your Story**
   If you're comfortable, share your journey of recognizing your need for Jesus and how He has brought healing and change into your life.

Conclusion

Jesus' statement in Matthew 9:12 is a profound declaration of His purpose to save those who recognize their need for Him. It challenges the self-righteous mindset and invites all, regardless of their past or present, to come to Him and be absolved. This passage encourages us to understand and embrace our need for the Great Physician and to extend His inclusive, healing love to others.

Theologians' Take

Theologians discuss this passage in the context of Jesus' radical grace and the nature of His kingdom. They note that Jesus' ministry consistently reached out to those on the fringes of society, challenging the religious norms of the day. Many emphasize that spiritual awareness of one's sickness is crucial for salvation and that Jesus' mission is centered on healing the spiritually broken. Theologians also reflect on the implications of this teaching for the church's mission, suggesting that it should continue to reflect Jesus' focus on reaching out to the sick and marginalized with compassion and grace.

Chapter 31 – New Wine into New Wineskins: Understanding 'The Bridegroom, Fasting, and Change'

This passage from Matthew 9:14-17 explores Jesus' response to questions about fasting. It is rich with symbolism and speaks to the nature of Jesus' mission and the new covenant He brings.

"Then John's disciples came and asked him, 'How is it that we and the Pharisees fast often, but your disciples do not fast?' Jesus answered, 'How can the guests of the bridegroom mourn while he is with them? The time will come when the bridegroom will be taken from them; then they will fast. No one sews a patch of unshrunk cloth on an old garment, for the patch will pull away from the garment, making the tear worse. Neither do people pour new wine into old wineskins. If they do, the skins will burst; the wine will run out and the wineskins will be ruined. No, they pour new wine into new wineskins, and both are preserved.'"

Understanding the Teaching

The above passage discusses the disciples of John the Baptist questioning Jesus about His disciples who do not fast often. Jesus first uses the metaphor of a wedding feast, indicating that His presence with His disciples is a time of celebration, not mourning. He then speaks of the incompatibility of new and old through the parables of unshrunk cloth on an old garment and new wine in old wineskins, emphasizing the need for receptivity to the new covenant He is establishing.

Key Points

1. **Time for Celebration**
   Jesus compares His time with His disciples to that of a wedding joy. This indicates that His presence is a reason for joy, not fasting.
2. **Incompatibility of Old and New**
   The old practices and structures cannot contain the new reality Jesus brings. Just as new wine requires new wineskins, His new covenant demands a fresh way of understanding and living.
3. **Transition and Transformation**
   Jesus is signaling a significant shift from the old covenant to the new, a transformation that involves rethinking the prevailing religious practices.
4. **Flexibility and Growth**
   The teachings about cloth and wineskins suggest that flexibility and openness to change are necessary to embrace the new things God is doing.
5. **Embracing the New Covenant**
   Jesus invites His followers to embrace the new covenant, characterized by grace, relationship, and the inner transformation of the heart.

Exercises to Apply This Teaching

1. **Reflect on Flexibility**
   Reflect on areas in your life where you might be resistant to change. Pray for an open and flexible heart to embrace what God is doing.
2. **Celebrate the Presence**
   Identify ways you can celebrate Jesus' presence in your life. It can be through worship, communion, or fellowship with other believers.

3. **Study the Covenants**
   Take time to study the different covenants in the Bible, noticing the transition from the old to the new covenant through Jesus.
4. **Embrace New Practices**
   Consider adopting a new spiritual practice that helps you freshly connect with God, reflecting the newness of life in Christ.
5. **Share the New Wine**
   Share with someone how Jesus has brought newness and transformation into your life, offering them encouragement and hope.

Conclusion

Jesus' teachings on fasting and the new covenant challenge us to rethink our religious practices and understandings in light of His transformative presence.

They invite us to embrace the newness He offers, a life characterized by joy, relationships, and inner change. This passage encourages us to be open to the new teachings of God, ensuring our hearts are receptive to new wineskins ready for the new wine of His kingdom.

Theologians' Take

Theologians discuss this passage in the context of the radical nature of Jesus' ministry and the transition from the old covenant of law to the new covenant of grace. They note that Jesus' message and actions frequently challenged existing religious norms, pushing His followers to a deeper understanding of God's intentions. Many theologians emphasize the importance of understanding and embracing the new covenant Jesus established, which fulfills and transcends the old. The new wine in new wineskins is seen as a metaphor for the transformative and renewing work of the Gospel, which requires fresh receptivity and openness from its adherents.

Chapter 32 – The Mission of the Twelve: Understanding 'The Instructions to the Disciples'

The passage from Matthew 10:5-42 explores the comprehensive instructions Jesus gives to His twelve disciples to go out on a mission. This passage is rich with guidance, warnings, and encouragement, providing a framework for understanding the mission and discipleship.

This extensive passage includes Jesus' detailed instructions to His twelve disciples as He sends them out to heal the sick, raise the dead, cleanse those with leprosy, drive out demons, and proclaim the kingdom of Heaven. He advises them on how to handle acceptance and rejection, warns them of persecution, encourages them with the promise of God's presence, and speaks of the cost and rewards of following Him.

Read the full passage at the end of this Chapter.

Understanding the Teaching

Jesus sends out His disciples with specific instructions, empowering them to heal the sick, raise the dead, cleanse those with leprosy, and exorcise demons.

He tells them to focus their efforts on the lost sheep of Israel and to rely on the hospitality of those they visit. He warns of persecution but encourages them with the promise of God's presence and guidance. Jesus speaks of the divisive nature of His message and the cost of discipleship, emphasizing the need for commitment and the rewards that come with it.

Key Points

1. **Empowerment for Service**
   The disciples are given authority to perform miraculous works, signifying the kingdom of God is at hand.
2. **Provision and Trust**
   They are instructed to take no provisions for the journey, relying instead on God and the generosity of those who receive them.
3. **Expectation of Persecution**
   Jesus warns that they will face opposition and even persecution, reflecting the cost of proclaiming the Gospel.
4. **Fearless Proclamation**
   Despite the dangers, the disciples are encouraged to speak boldly and fearlessly, trusting that the Holy Spirit will guide them.
5. **Cost and Reward of Discipleship**
   Following Jesus may lead to division and sacrifice, but it also comes with the promise of eternal rewards.

Exercises to Apply This Teaching

1. **Identify Your 'Lost Sheep'**
   Reflect on who in your community might be considered the lost sheep. Consider ways you can reach out to them with compassion and service.
2. **Practice Dependence on God**
   Choose a day to consciously rely on God for something you would usually depend on yourself or others for, strengthening your trust in Him.
3. **Courage in Witnessing**
   Identify an opportunity to share your faith or speak up about an issue important to you. Pray to have clarity and courage.

4. **Reflect on Persecution**
   Educate yourself on the persecution Christians face globally.
   Pray for them and consider how you can support persecuted
   believers.
5. **Count the Cost**
   Reflect on the cost of discipleship in your life. Are there
   areas where you need to make a deeper commitment to
   follow Jesus?

Conclusion

The instructions to the twelve disciples in chapter 10 of Matthew
provide a powerful blueprint for mission and discipleship.

It reminds us of the empowerment, provision, challenges, and
ultimate rewards we get for following Jesus and participating in His
work. This passage encourages us to embrace our calling with
courage, reliance on God, and a commitment to the cost and joys of
discipleship.

Theologians' Take

Theologians discuss this passage as a foundational text for
understanding Christian mission and evangelism. They note the
balance between the authority given to the disciples and their
vulnerability and dependence on God and others. Theologians
reflect on the nature of Christian witness, often focusing on the
promise of divine presence and guidance amidst opposition.

The passage is also seen as a call to radical discipleship, challenging
believers to consider the depth of their commitment to following
Christ. Many emphasize that the mission of the disciples is not just a
historical event but a continuing call to the church today, inviting
ongoing engagement with the world in proclaiming and embodying
the Gospel.

The Twelve Apostles- These twelve Jesus sent out with the following instructions:

"These twelve Jesus sent out with the following instructions: 'Do not go among the Gentiles or enter any town of the Samaritans. Go rather to the lost sheep of Israel. As you go, proclaim this message: 'The kingdom of heaven has come near.' Heal the sick, raise the dead, cleanse those who have leprosy, drive out demons. Freely you have received; freely give.'

'Do not get any gold or silver or copper to take with you in your belts—no bag for the journey or extra shirt or sandals or a staff, for the worker is worth his keep. Whatever town or village you enter, search there for some worthy person and stay at their house until you leave. As you enter the home, give it your greeting. If the home is deserving, let your peace rest on it; if it is not, let your peace return to you. If anyone will not welcome you or listen to your words, leave that home or town and shake the dust off your feet. Truly I tell you, it will be more bearable for Sodom and Gomorrah on the day of judgment than for that town.'

'I am sending you out like sheep among wolves. Therefore be as shrewd as snakes and as innocent as doves. Be on your guard; you will be handed over to the local councils and be flogged in the synagogues. On my account you will be brought before governors and kings as witnesses to them and to the Gentiles. But when they arrest you, do not worry about what to say or how to say it. At that time you will be given what to say, for it will not be you speaking, but the Spirit of your Father speaking through you.'

'Brother will betray brother to death, and a father his child; children will rebel against their parents and have them put to death. You will be hated by everyone because of me, but the one who stands firm to the end will be saved. When you are persecuted in one place, flee to another. Truly I tell you, you will not finish going through the towns of Israel before the Son of Man comes.'

'The student is not above the teacher, nor a servant above his master. It is enough for students to be like their teachers, and servants like their masters. If the head of the house has been called Beelzebul, how much more the members of his household!'

'So do not be afraid of them, for there is nothing concealed that will not be disclosed, or hidden that will not be made known. What I tell you in the dark, speak in the daylight; what is whispered in your ear, proclaim from the roofs. Do not be afraid of those who kill the body but cannot kill the soul. Rather, be afraid of the One who can destroy both soul and body in hell. Are not two sparrows sold for a penny? Yet not one of them will fall to the ground outside your Father's care. And even the very hairs of your head are all numbered. So don't be afraid; you are worth more than many sparrows.'

'Whoever acknowledges me before others, I will also acknowledge before my Father in heaven. But whoever disowns me before others, I will disown before my Father in heaven.'

'Do not suppose that I have come to bring peace to the earth. I did not come to bring peace, but a sword. For I have come to turn

'a man against his father,

a daughter against her mother,

a daughter-in-law against her mother-in-law—

a man's enemies will be the members of his own household.''

'Anyone who loves their father or mother more than me is not worthy of me; anyone who loves their son or daughter more than me is not worthy of me. Whoever does not take up their cross and follow me is not worthy of me. Whoever finds their life will lose it, and whoever loses their life for my sake will find it.'

'Anyone who welcomes you welcomes me, and anyone who welcomes me welcomes the one who sent me. Whoever welcomes a prophet as a prophet will receive a prophet's reward, and whoever welcomes a righteous person as a righteous person will receive a righteous person's reward. And if anyone gives even a cup of cold water to one of these little ones who is my disciple, truly I tell you, that person will certainly not lose their reward.'"

Chapter 33 – Jesus and John the Baptist

In this chapter, we explore a significant passage where Jesus responds to inquiries from John the Baptist and addresses the crowd about John's role. This section of Matthew 11 (verses 4-19) provides insight into how Jesus' works affirm His identity and how people's responses vary to His and John's ministries.

See the whole Passage Matthew 11:4-19 at the end of the chapter.

Understanding the Teaching

John the Baptist, imprisoned at the time, sends his disciples to ask Jesus if He is the one who is to come. Jesus responds not with a direct claim but by citing the evidence of His works: the blind receive sight, the boring walk, the lepers are cleansed, the deaf hear, the dead are raised, and the good news is proclaimed to the poor. Jesus then discusses John's role as a prophet and more while also commenting on the fickle and contradictory responses of the people to both His and John's ministries.

Key Points

1. **Evidence of Messiahship**
   Jesus' miracles serve as fulfillment of messianic prophecies, affirming His identity as the Messiah.
2. **Blessed are the Unoffended**
   Jesus pronounces a blessing on those who do not fall away on account of Him, encouraging open-hearted acceptance of His sometimes challenging teachings and actions.
3. **John's Role Affirmed**
   Jesus confirms John's prophetic role and identifies him as the Elijah who was to come, affirming his importance and ministry.

116

4. **Inconsistent Responses**
   Jesus critiques the generation for their inconsistent responses - they were dissatisfied with both John's asceticism and Jesus' engagement with society.
5. **Wisdom Vindicated by Deeds**
   Jesus concludes that wisdom is proved right by actions, suggesting that the fruits of one's life validate one's path.

Exercises to Apply This Teaching

1. **Reflect on Your Response**
   Reflect on how you have responded to Jesus in your own life. Are there teachings or aspects of His character you find difficult to accept? Pray for openness and understanding.
2. **Miracles Today**
   Identify and document stories or personal experiences that testify to God's work today, whether they are miraculous healings or transformative acts of kindness.
3. **Role of Prophets**
   Study the role of prophets in the Bible. Consider how their messages were received and what that teaches about receiving challenging or countercultural messages today.
4. **Wisdom in Action**
   Choose a teaching of Jesus and consciously apply it in your life for a week. Observe the effects and reflect on the wisdom it reveals.
5. **Bless Others**
   Be a source of good news, especially to those who are disadvantaged or suffering. You can volunteer, donate, or simply offer a listening ear and a kind word.

Conclusion

Matthew 11:4-19 challenges us to consider our response to Jesus and His works. It encourages us to look beyond our expectations and prejudices and to see the evidence of His identity in His deeds and teachings. The passage invites us to a blessed life of unoffended faith, recognizing the true roles of God's messengers and validating wisdom through righteous actions.

Theologians' Take

Theologians discuss this passage in the context of messianic expectations and the fulfillment of prophecy. They note Jesus' strategic use of miracles and teachings as evidence of His identity, reflecting the prophetic descriptions of the Messiah's work.

Theologians also reflect on the nature of the offense in relation to Jesus, suggesting that His mission and message often challenge established norms and expectations, causing various reactions. The discussion about John the Baptist's role as Elijah highlights the continuity and fulfillment of God's redemptive plan. In general, theologians consider this passage crucial for comprehending Jesus' self-revelation and the diverse human responses to His person and work.

Jesus replied, "Go back and report to John what you hear and see: The blind receive sight, the lame walk, those who have leprosy are cleansed, the deaf hear, the dead are raised, and the good news is proclaimed to the poor. Blessed is anyone who does not stumble on account of me."

As John's disciples were leaving, Jesus began to speak to the crowd about John: "What did you go out into the wilderness to see? A reed swayed by the wind? If not, what did you go out to see? A man dressed in fine clothes? No, those who wear fine clothes are in kings' palaces. Then what did you go out to see? A prophet? Yes, I tell you, and more than a prophet. This is the one about whom it is written:

" 'I will send my messenger ahead of you,

who will prepare your way before you.'

Truly I tell you, among those born of women there has not risen anyone greater than John the Baptist; yet whoever is least in the kingdom of heaven is greater than he.

From the days of John the Baptist until now, the kingdom of heaven has been subjected to violence, and violent people have been raiding it. For all the Prophets and the Law prophesied until John. And if you are willing to accept it, he is the Elijah who was to come. Whoever has ears, let them hear.

"To what can I compare this generation? They are like children sitting in the marketplaces and calling out to others:

" 'We played the pipe for you,

and you did not dance;

we sang a dirge,

and you did not mourn.'

For John came neither eating nor drinking, and they say, 'He has a demon.' The Son of Man came eating and drinking, and they say, 'Here is a glutton and a drunkard, a friend of tax collectors and sinners.' But wisdom is proved right by her deeds."

Chapter 34 – The Call to Repentance: Understanding 'Woe to Unrepentant Towns'

In Matthew 11:21-24, we examine Jesus' pronouncement of woe on the unrepentant towns. Jesus rebuked the cities in which most of his miracles were performed because they did not repent.

"Woe to you, Chorazin! Woe to you, Bethsaida! For if the miracles that were performed in you had been performed in Tyre and Sidon, they would have repented long ago in sackcloth and ashes. But I tell you, it will be more bearable for Tyre and Sidon on the day of judgment than for you. And you, Capernaum, will you be lifted to the heavens? No, you will go down to Hades. For if the miracles that were performed in you had been performed in Sodom, it would have remained to this day. But I tell you that it will be more bearable for Sodom on the day of judgment than for you."

Understanding the Teaching

Jesus criticizes the cities of Chorazin, Bethsaida, and Capernaum for their failure to turn back to God despite witnessing His miraculous works. He suggests that if the pagan cities of Tyre, Sidon, and Sodom had seen such miracles, they would have repented long ago.

The punishment for these unrepentant cities is clear: they will face a harsher outcome than the notoriously sinful cities known from the Old Testament.

Key Points

1. **Miracles as Calls to Repentance**
   Jesus sees His miracles not just as acts of compassion but as invitations to transformation and repentance.

2. **Responsibility to Respond**
   Witnessing God's works increases the responsibility to respond appropriately, and indifference leads to greater judgment.
3. **The Severity of Judgment**
   The comparison to Tyre, Sidon, and Sodom underlines the seriousness of ignoring the call to repentance.
4. **Privilege and Accountability**
   Being privileged garners responsibility, and the cities that were fortunate to witness Jesus' miracles were held accountable for their response.
5. **Repentance as a Priority**
   The core message of Jesus' ministry is the call to repent and realign one's life with the kingdom of God.

Exercises to Apply This Teaching

1. **Evaluate Your Response**
   Reflect on how you have responded to God's work in your life. Are there areas where you've been indifferent or resistant to change?
2. **Practice Repentance**
   Identify a specific area you need to turn away from. Take practical steps to change direction and seek accountability.
3. **Learn from History**
   Study the historical context of Tyre, Sidon, and Sodom to understand the gravity of Jesus' comparison. Reflect on the importance of heeding warnings and learning from the past.

4. **Pray for Insight**
   Pray for insight into the miracles or blessings you may have overlooked. Ask for a heart that is responsive and repentant.
5. **Community Action**
   Engage with your community in discussing how you collectively might need to heed calls for repentance. Consider actions that can be taken to foster transformation.

Conclusion

Matthew 11:21-24 highlights the critical nature of repentance in response to Jesus' ministry. It warns of the consequences of ignoring such a call and serves as a stark reminder that privilege comes with responsibility. This chapter calls us to acknowledge God's work in our lives and to live in a way that reflects genuine transformation and alignment with God's will.

Theologians' Take

Theologians interpret this passage as emphasizing the justice of God in the face of human stubbornness. They discuss the balance between God's mercy, shown in Jesus' miracles, and His justice, evidenced in the call to repentance and the warning of judgment. This passage is also a sobering reminder of the importance of responding to God's gracious acts with genuine repentance. Theologians caution against taking God's grace for granted and highlight the importance of repentance as a continuous, integral part of the Christian life.

Chapter 35 – The Gentle Mastery of Christ: Understanding 'The Father Revealed in the Son'

In this chapter, we explore Jesus' profound thanksgiving and invitation as recorded in Matthew 11:25-30. He reveals the intimate relationship between the Father and the Son and extends a call to find rest in Him.

"At that time Jesus said, 'I praise you, Father, Lord of heaven and earth, because you have hidden these things from the wise and learned, and revealed them to little children. Yes, Father, for this is what you were pleased to do. All things have been committed to me by my Father. No one knows the Son except the Father, and no one knows the Father except the Son and those to whom the Son chooses to reveal him. Come to me, all you who are weary and burdened, and I will give you rest. Take my yoke upon you and learn from me, for I am gentle and humble in heart, and you will find rest for your souls. For my yoke is easy and my burden is light.'"

Understanding the Teaching

Jesus expresses gratitude to God for revealing the truths of the kingdom to "little children" — those with open, humble hearts — rather than to the wise and learned.

He states that only the Son knows the Father and only those to whom the Son chooses to reveal Him. Jesus then invites all who are weary and burdened to come to Him for rest, offering His gentle and humble heart as a model. He tells everyone that His yoke is easy to use and the burden He carries is light, in contrast to the heavy burdens placed by religious leaders of the time.

A yoke is a wooden beam traditionally used between a pair of oxen to enable them to pull together on a load when working in fields. In the context of what Jesus is referring to, the yoke is a metaphor for the burdens or obligations that are placed upon someone.

When Jesus speaks of His yoke, He contrasts it with the heavy, burdensome religious laws and social expectations that were placed upon the people by religious leaders of the time. The religious leaders' yoke could be seen as a set of strict, legalistic interpretations of the Law of Moses, which could be oppressive and difficult to bear.

Jesus invites people to take His yoke upon them, suggesting a different kind of burden, one that is easy and light. In essence, Jesus is offering a new way to relate to God, not through the heavy burden of legalistic demands, but through a relationship of love, grace, and mercy. His teachings provide guidance that is meant to be liberating rather than oppressive. By following Jesus and learning from Him, believers find rest for their souls because His teachings and way of life are meant to be fulfilling and life-giving. Jesus emphasizes humility and gentleness as part of this yoke, which contrasts with the harsh and prideful ways religious burdens were sometimes imposed.

So, when Jesus talks about His yoke being easy and His burden light, He is referring to the teachings and commandments He gives, which are rooted in love and meant to be manageable. This is in contrast to the heavy and often impossible-to-bear burdens of legalistic religious law. Jesus is promising a life that is spiritually rich and freeing, not because it is without obligation or effort, but because it is aligned with true righteousness, peace, and joy in the Holy Spirit.

Key Points

1. **Divine Revelation**
   The Father reveals the truths of the kingdom to those with childlike openness, not through human wisdom.
2. **Exclusive Knowledge**
   Jesus has exclusive knowledge of the Father, and only through Jesus can the Father be fully known.
3. **Invitation to Rest**
   Jesus invites those weary from life's burdens to find rest in Him, offering a relationship rather than a religion.
4. **Easy Yoke and Light Burden**
   Jesus' way of life — His yoke — is not burdensome but is characterized by grace and peace.
5. **The Heart of Christ**
   Jesus is gentle and humble, and in taking on His yoke, His followers are to emulate these qualities.

Exercises to Apply This Teaching

1. **Childlike Faith**
   Approaching God with childlike faith, which is pure and innocent. Spend time in prayer or nature, allowing yourself to marvel and wonder without overanalyzing.
2. **Yoke Reflection**
   Reflect on what burdens you may be carrying that Jesus did not intend for you. Consider how you can lay them down and take up Jesus' yoke instead.
3. **Rest in Christ**
   Intentionally take time to rest in Christ's presence. This could be through quiet meditation, reading scripture, or listening to hymns or carols.
4. **Learn from Jesus**
   Study the character and actions of Jesus in the Gospels. Identify ways you can emulate His gentleness and humility in your daily life.

5. **Community Encouragement**
   Share the invitation of Jesus with someone who is burdened. Offer to pray for them or practically help them.

Conclusion

Matthew 11:25-30 provides a comforting assurance of the intimate knowledge and restful leadership of Jesus. It invites us to a life of simplicity, humility, and rest in the knowledge of God as revealed by Jesus. The passage calls us away from self-reliant struggle and toward a grace-filled existence under the gentle mastery of Christ.

Theologians' Take

Theologians discuss divine revelation and the nature of discipleship in this passage. They note that Jesus' teachings turn societal and religious expectations upside down — valuing humility over pride and rest over labor. This passage is frequently highlighted in discussions of soteriology, the study of salvation, emphasizing that knowing God and finding rest for the soul is possible only through Christ. Theologians also point to the easy yoke as a metaphor for discipleship that is not burdensome but is sustained by the grace and love of Jesus.

Chapter 36 – The Lord of the Sabbath: Understanding Compassion Over Ceremony

This chapter contains verses from Matthew 12:3-8 and 11-13, which discuss teachings about the Sabbath. Jesus responds to Pharisaic's criticism of His disciples for plucking grain on the Sabbath by citing scriptural precedents and emphasizing the spirit of the law over the letter.

"He answered, 'Haven't you read what David did when he and his companions were hungry? He entered the house of God, and he and his companions ate the consecrated bread—which was not lawful for them to do, but only for the priests. Or haven't you read in the Law that the priests on Sabbath duty in the temple desecrate the Sabbath and yet are innocent? I tell you that something greater than the temple is here. If you had known what these words mean, 'I desire mercy, not sacrifice,' you would not have condemned the innocent. For the Son of Man is Lord of the Sabbath.'

[...] He said to them, 'If any of you has a sheep and it falls into a pit on the Sabbath, will you not take hold of it and lift it out? How much more valuable is a person than a sheep! Therefore, it is lawful to do good on the Sabbath.' Then he said to the man, 'Stretch out your hand.' So he stretched it out and it was completely restored, just as sound as the other.'"

Understanding the Teaching

When the Pharisees accuse Jesus' disciples of breaking the Sabbath by picking grain to eat, Jesus recalls the event when David ate the consecrated bread and the priests who worked in the temple on the Sabbath. He emphasizes that mercy is more important than sacrifice and proclaims Himself as Lord of the Sabbath, suggesting His authority to interpret and fulfill the law. Jesus further illustrates His point by healing a man with a shriveled hand on the Sabbath, highlighting the Law's intent to promote good rather than hinder it.

Key Points

1. **Compassion Over Legalism**
   Jesus teaches that compassionate deeds are in harmony with the Sabbath's purpose, which is to benefit and restore life.
2. **Lordship Over the Sabbath**
   Jesus' claim to be Lord of the Sabbath asserts His divine authority to interpret the true meaning of the Law.
3. **Law's Intent for Good**
   The Law was given to promote well-being, not to be an oppressive burden. Jesus corrects the misapplication of the Sabbath law.
4. **Mercy as a Priority**
   Jesus prioritizes acts of mercy and kindness over rigid adherence to religious rituals or ceremonies.
5. **Doing Good on the Sabbath**
   By healing the man's hand, Jesus demonstrates that doing good and meeting needs is always lawful, even on the Sabbath.

Exercises to Apply This Teaching

1. **Reflect on Rest and Restoration**
   Consider how you observe rest and restoration in your own life. Are your practices legalistic, or do they reflect the therapeutic intent of the Sabbath?
2. **Mercy in Action**
   Identify an opportunity to perform an act of mercy, even if it's during your time of rest. Note how it aligns with the spirit of the Sabbath.

3. **Study Sabbath Laws**
   Study the laws regarding the Sabbath in the Old Testament and how Jesus fulfills them. Reflect on their significance in your life.
4. **Address Legalism**
   Consider if there are aspects of your faith practice that have become legalistic. Pray and seek counsel on how to bring them back to the heart of worship.
5. **Share Healing and Rest**
   Offer assistance to someone in need, symbolizing the healing Jesus performed on the Sabbath, and share the rest and peace found in Christ.

Conclusion

Matthew 12:3-8 and 11-13 reframe the concept of the Sabbath, shifting the focus from strict legalistic observance to the underlying principles of mercy, compassion, and doing good. Jesus, as Lord of the Sabbath, invites us to a deeper understanding of rest that aligns with God's intentions for human flourishing. This passage encourages us to live out the spirit of the Sabbath every day by prioritizing acts of mercy and kindness over ritualistic obligations.

Theologians' Take

Theologians explore this passage as a revelation of Jesus' authority and His interpretive principles regarding the Law. They note that Jesus does not dismiss the Sabbath but reclaims it, emphasizing its purpose to serve humanity's needs and God's desire for mercy rather than sacrifice. Jesus' actions on the Sabbath are seen as enactments of the kingdom of God, where human need takes precedence over ceremonial law. Theologians also discuss the implications of Jesus' lordship for contemporary Christian practice, suggesting that it calls for a compassionate and life-giving observance of rest and worship.

Chapter 37 – Integrity of the Kingdom: Understanding 'God's Chosen Servant'

In Matthew 12:25-37, which includes Jesus' response to the Pharisees' accusation of demonic collaboration, Jesus warns about the unforgivable sin and the importance of one's words in revealing one's spiritual state.

See the entire passage of Matthew 12:25-37 and the end of the chapter.

Understanding the Teaching

Jesus counters the Pharisees' claims that He casts out demons by the power of Beelzebul. He explains that a kingdom divided against itself cannot stand, highlighting the illogical nature of their accusation. He then addresses the blasphemy against the Holy Spirit, warning that while every sin can be forgiven, blasphemy against the Spirit will not be forgiven. Jesus also underscores the importance of integrity, stating that a good tree cannot bear bad fruit and vice versa. Finally, He emphasizes the importance of words, asserting that people will be judged by their spoken words, which reflect the condition of their hearts.

Key Points

1. **Unity and Consistency**
   A kingdom must be united to survive, and Jesus' works of healing and deliverance are consistent with the kingdom of God's values.

2. **Blasphemy of the Holy Spirit**
   This sin involves attributing the Spirit's holy work through Jesus to an evil source, a profound and stubborn rejection of God's grace.
3. **Fruits of the Heart**
   Our actions and words are the fruits that demonstrate the true nature of our hearts, whether good or evil.
4. **Responsibility of Speech**
   Words are not neutral; they carry weight and reveal one's inner righteousness or wickedness.
5. **Judgment and Justification**
   Our words can either absolve or condemn us, as they are the outflow of our hearts and will be the basis for judgment.

Exercises to Apply This Teaching

1. **Self-Reflection on Unity**
   Reflect on how you contribute to unity or division within your family, church, or community. Pledge to actions that build unity.
2. **Guarding Against Blasphemy**
   Be cautious about making quick judgments on the work of others, especially when they claim to be led by the Spirit. Pray for discernment and humility.
3. **Fruit Inspection**
   Examine the fruits of your life—your actions and your words. Ask for God's help to remove anything that doesn't honor Him.
4. **Mind Your Words**
   Practice mindfulness in speech. Before speaking, consider if your words will reflect well on your character and faith.
5. **Accountability in Speech**
   Partner with a trusted friend or family member to hold each other accountable for the words you speak.

Conclusion

Matthew 12:25-37 calls us to a life of integrity, where our spoken words and actions reflect the kingdom of God. It warns against the dangers of a divided life and the profound consequences of our attitudes towards God's Spirit. This chapter encourages us to cultivate a heart that produces good fruit and to use our speech for justice and blessing rather than harm.

Theologians' Take

Theologians explore this passage with an emphasis on the nature of Jesus' mission—His divine authority over evil and His ushering in God's kingdom. The discussion on the unforgivable sin of blasphemy against the Holy Spirit is heavily debated, with a common view being that it represents a willful, persistent rejection of God's grace. Theologians also focus on the ethical implications of Jesus' teachings about the fruits of the heart and the significance of words, viewing them as a reflection of one's true spiritual condition and a vital aspect of Christian witness and life.

"Jesus knew their thoughts and said to them, 'Every kingdom divided against itself will be ruined, and every city or household divided against itself will not stand. If Satan drives out Satan, he is divided against himself. How then can his kingdom stand? And if I drive out demons by Beelzebul, by whom do your people drive them out? So then, they will be your judges. But if it is by the Spirit of God that I drive out demons, then the kingdom of God has come upon you.'"

"Or again, how can anyone enter a strong man's house and carry off his possessions unless he first ties up the strong man? Then he can plunder his house."

"Whoever is not with me is against me, and whoever does not gather with me scatters. And so I tell you, every kind of sin and slander can

be forgiven, but blasphemy against the Spirit will not be forgiven. Anyone who speaks a word against the Son of Man will be forgiven, but anyone who speaks against the Holy Spirit will not be forgiven, either in this age or in the age to come."

"Make a tree good and its fruit will be good, or make a tree bad and its fruit will be bad, for a tree is recognized by its fruit. You brood of vipers, how can you who are evil say anything good? For the mouth speaks what the heart is full of. A good man brings good things out of the good stored up in him, and an evil man brings evil things out of the evil stored up in him. But I tell you that everyone will have to give account on the day of judgment for every empty word they have spoken. For by your words you will be acquitted, and by your words you will be condemned."

Chapter 38 – The Sign of Jonah: Understanding a Call for Repentance

In this chapter of Matthew 12:39-45, we reflect on Jesus' response to the demand for a sign. Jesus speaks about the Sign of Jonah, connecting His resurrection with Jonah's symbolic entombment and deliverance.

He answered, "A wicked and adulterous generation asks for a sign! But none will be given it except the sign of the prophet Jonah. For as Jonah was three days and three nights in the belly of a huge fish, so the Son of Man will be three days and three nights in the heart of the earth. The men of Nineveh will stand up at the judgment with this generation and condemn it; for they repented at the preaching of Jonah, and now something greater than Jonah is here. The Queen of the South will rise at the judgment with this generation and condemn it; for she came from the ends of the earth to listen to Solomon's wisdom, and now something greater than Solomon is here.

"When an impure spirit comes out of a person, it goes through arid places seeking rest and does not find it. Then it says, 'I will return to the house I left.' When it arrives, it finds the house unoccupied, swept clean and put in order. Then it goes and takes with it seven other spirits more wicked than itself, and they go in and live there. And the final condition of that person is worse than the first. That is how it will be with this wicked generation."

Understanding the Teaching

When the Pharisees and teachers of the law ask Jesus for a sign, He tells them that no sign will be given except the Sign of Jonah. Just as Jonah was in the belly of a great fish for three days and nights, so will the Son of Man be in the heart of the Earth. Jesus uses this sign to foretell His death and resurrection. He also criticizes the current generation for their unbelief, contrasting their response to that of the Ninevites, who repented at Jonah's preaching and the Queen of the South, who sought Solomon's wisdom.

Key Points

1. **The Sign of Resurrection**
   The Sign of Jonah symbolizes Jesus' resurrection, the ultimate proof of His divine authority and mission.
2. **Repentance is Key**
   The people of Nineveh responded to Jonah's warning with repentance, which Jesus highlights to call His contemporaries to repentance.
3. **A Greater Than Jonah**
   Jesus indicates that something greater than Jonah is here, referring to Himself and the greater call to repentance He brings.
4. **Seeking Wisdom**
   The Queen of the South's quest for wisdom underscores the value of seeking truth and recognizing wisdom in Jesus' teachings.
5. **Judgment for Unbelief**
   The generation's refusal to heed Jesus' message will lead to judgment, as exemplified by the Ninevites and the Queen, who responded rightly to lesser revelations.

Exercises to Apply This Teaching

1. **Reflect on Your 'Signs'**
   Consider the signs or evidence in your life that affirm Jesus' teachings. Are you seeking more signs, or are you responding to what has already been revealed?
2. **Act of Repentance**
   Identify an area in your life that requires repentance. Take tangible steps towards making amends and changing your behavior.

3. **Wisdom Search**
   Engage with the Gospels, seeking the wisdom of Jesus as the Queen of the South sought Solomon's. Document insights and how they can be applied in your life.
4. **Share the Message**
   Emulate Jonah by sharing the message of repentance and redemption with others. This could be through personal testimony or community service.
5. **Evaluate Your Response**
   Journal about your response to Jesus' message. Are you indifferent, or are you actively living out the teachings of Christ?

Conclusion

Matthew 12:39-45 serves as a plain reminder that the greatest sign has already been given through Jesus' resurrection. The call to repentance is urgent and demands a response. This passage challenges us to evaluate our reaction to Jesus' message, encouraging us to seek wisdom and live a life of repentance and faithfulness.

Theologians' Take

Theologians view the Sign of Jonah as a typological foreshadowing of Jesus' death and resurrection. They discuss the necessity of repentance in response to divine revelation, as seen in the Ninevites' reaction to Jonah's preaching. This passage is commonly interpreted as a critique of those seeking signs rather than responding to the message of the Gospel. Theologians underscore the sufficiency of Jesus' resurrection as the foundational sign for believers and the basis for Christian hope and life transformation.

Chapter 39 – The Parable of the Sower: Understanding the Receptivity of Our Hearts

In chapter 13:1-9 of Matthew, the Parable of the Sower is discussed. This parable is a profound illustration of how the message of the kingdom of God is received differently by people based on the condition of their hearts.

That same day Jesus went out of the house and sat by the lake. Such large crowds gathered around him that he got into a boat and sat in it, while all the people stood on the shore. Then he told them many things in parables, saying: "A farmer went out to sow his seed. As he was scattering the seed, some fell along the path, and the birds came and ate it up. Some fell on rocky places, where it did not have much soil. It sprang up quickly because the soil was shallow. But when the sun came up, the plants were scorched, and they withered because they had no root. Other seed fell among thorns, which grew up and choked the plants. Still other seed fell on good soil, where it produced a crop—a hundred, sixty or thirty times what was sown. Whoever has ears, let them hear."

Understanding the Teaching

Jesus describes a sower who scatters seeds. Some seeds fall along the path and are eaten by birds. Others fall on rocky places where they don't have much soil; these seeds spring up quickly but wither because they have no roots. Other seeds fall among thorns, which grow up and choke the plants. Finally, some seeds fall on good soil, where they produce a crop that is several times more than what was sown.

Key Points

1. **The Path**
   Represents those who hear the message of the kingdom but do not understand it, allowing the evil one to snatch away what was sown in their hearts.
2. **Rocky Ground**
   Symbolizes those who receive the message with joy but disperse when trouble or persecution is encountered because they lack a firm root.
3. **Among Thorns**
   Depicts those who hear the word, but the concerns of this life and the deceitfulness of wealth suffocate it, rendering it unfruitful.
4. **Good Soil**
   Depicts those who hear the word and understand it, leading to a life that produces a rich harvest.

Exercises to Apply This Teaching

1. **Soil Assessment**
   Reflect on the state of your soil — heart. Are there areas in your life that resemble rocky places or thorny paths? Take steps to cultivate them into good soil.
2. **Root Development**
   Engage in practices that deepen your spiritual roots, like regular study of the Scriptures, prayer, and joining a community of faith for support and growth.
3. **Thorn Removal**
   Identify and address the thorns in your life—worries, wealth, ambitions—that might be choking your spiritual growth. Consider what changes you can make to prioritize your spiritual well-being.

4. **Harvest Actions**
   Actively seek to understand and apply the teachings of Jesus in your daily life. Look for ways to share your faith and serve others as part of producing a fruitful harvest.
5. **Yield Journaling**
   Keep a journal of how you are applying the word of God in your life and the fruit it is producing. Reflect on the growth and the areas that still need cultivation.

Conclusion

The Parable of the Sower invites us to examine the receptivity of our hearts to the message of God's kingdom. It encourages us not only to listen to the word but also to understand and integrate it into our lives, bearing fruit in accordance with our faith. Our response to the word can determine the spiritual yield of our lives, reminding us of the importance of cultivating a heart open and receptive to God's teachings.

Theologians' Take

Theologians interpret the Parable of the Sower as a representation of the varied responses to the Gospel's message. It's a challenge to the hearer to be self-reflective and strive towards becoming better. Theologians point out that the parable emphasizes both the sovereign work of God in giving growth and the responsibility of hearers to hear well. It's also noted that the fruit isn't just personal holiness. Still, it includes mission and witness, as the good soil not only receives the word but also multiplies it, impacting the wider community.

Chapter 40 – The Purpose of Parables: Gaining Insight into the Kingdom

In Matthew 13:10-23, Jesus explains why He uses parables to teach the people and provides an interpretation of the Parable of the Sower.

See the whole passage at the end of the chapter.

Understanding the Teaching

Jesus employs parables to convey spiritual truths, but the disciples question why He speaks to the crowds in such a roundabout way. Jesus explains that the knowledge of the secrets of the kingdom of heaven has been given to the disciples only.

He quotes Isaiah, suggesting that the people's hearts have become hard; they hardly hear with their ears, and they have closed their eyes. Jesus then explains the Parable of the Sower, clarifying the different types of responses people have to the word of the kingdom.

Key Points

1. **Privilege of Understanding**
   The disciples are given direct explanations of spiritual truths, a privilege that comes with their close relationship with Jesus.
2. **Spiritual Receptivity**
   Parables reveal the state of the hearers' hearts—only those with open hearts will truly understand and accept the message.

3. **Fulfillment of Prophecy**
   Jesus' use of parables fulfills the prophecy that not everyone
   will understand or accept His teachings.
4. **Interpretation of the Sower**
   Jesus breaks down the Parable of the Sower, explaining each
   type of soil as a metaphor for the condition of people's hearts
   when they hear the word of the kingdom.
5. **Blessed are the Seeing and Hearing**
   Those who see the truths in Jesus' teachings and hear His
   message are blessed because many prophets and righteous
   people have longed for such understanding.

Exercises to Apply This Teaching

1. **Assess Your Heart-Soil**
   Reflect on how you receive spiritual teachings. Are you open
   and understanding, or are you indifferent and dismissive?
2. **Seek Deeper Understanding**
   Choose one of Jesus' parables and spend time studying it,
   looking for the deeper meaning behind it.
3. **Nurture Spiritual Growth**
   Like the good soil, make a conscious effort to nurture
   spiritual growth in yourself through practices like prayer,
   meditation, and community worship.
4. **Share Insights**
   Discuss a parable with friends or a study group and share
   your insights and interpretations to help each other grow in
   understanding.
5. **Apply Parable Lessons**
   Identify a lesson from a parable and find a way to apply it to
   your life this week, reflecting Jesus' teachings in your
   actions.

Conclusion

Matthew 13:10-23 demonstrates that while parables may seem enigmatic, they are a tool to discern the readiness of the heart. Jesus teaches that a true understanding of the kingdom comes not just from hearing words but from perceiving and internalizing their deeper meanings.

This passage challenges us to examine our receptivity to divine truth and to seek the blessed understanding that comes from a close relationship with Jesus.

Theologians' Take

Theologians view Jesus' use of parables as a means to both reveal and conceal truth. Parables are seen as a judgment against the willfully blind but also as mercy, offering an obscure invitation to those not yet ready for direct truth. The explanation of the sower is seen as key to understanding all parables, as it lays out the different responses to Jesus' teachings. Theologians also discuss the responsibility that comes with understanding—those who understand are called to bear fruit in keeping with the message of the kingdom.

The disciples came to him and asked, "Why do you speak to the people in parables?"

He replied, "Because the knowledge of the secrets of the kingdom of heaven has been given to you, but not to them. Whoever has will be given more, and they will have an abundance. Whoever does not have, even what they have will be taken from them. This is why I speak to them in parables:

Though seeing, they do not see;

though hearing, they do not hear or understand.

In them is fulfilled the prophecy of Isaiah:

" 'You will be ever hearing but never understanding;

you will be ever seeing but never perceiving.

For this people's heart has become calloused;

they hardly hear with their ears,

and they have closed their eyes.

Otherwise they might see with their eyes,

hear with their ears,

understand with their hearts

and turn, and I would heal them. '

But blessed are your eyes because they see, and your ears because they hear. For truly I tell you, many prophets and righteous people longed to see what you see but did not see it, and to hear what you hear but did not hear it.

"Listen then to what the parable of the sower means: When anyone hears the message about the kingdom and does not understand it, the evil one comes and snatches away what was sown in their heart. This is the seed sown along the path. The seed falling on rocky ground refers to someone who hears the word and at once receives it with joy. But since they have no root, they last only a short time. When trouble or persecution comes because of the word, they quickly fall away. The seed falling among the thorns refers to someone who hears the word, but the worries of this life and the deceitfulness of wealth choke the word, making it unfruitful. But the seed falling on good soil refers to someone who hears the word and

understands it. This is the one who produces a crop, yielding a hundred, sixty or thirty times what was sown."

Chapter 41 – The Parable of the Weeds: Understanding Coexistence and Judgment

In chapter 13 of the book of Matthew verse 24-30, Jesus shares the Parable of the Weeds, offering profound insights into the coexistence of good and evil in the word and the concept of final judgment.

"Jesus told them another parable: 'The kingdom of heaven is like a man who sowed good seed in his field. But while everyone was sleeping, his enemy came and sowed weeds among the wheat, and went away. When the wheat sprouted and formed heads, then the weeds also appeared.

'The owner's servants came to him and said, 'Sir, didn't you sow good seed in your field? Where then did the weeds come from?'

'An enemy did this,' he replied.

The servants asked him, 'Do you want us to go and pull them up?'

'No,' he answered, 'because while you are pulling the weeds, you may uproot the wheat with them. Let both grow together until the harvest. At that time I will tell the harvesters: First collect the weeds and tie them in bundles to be burned; then gather the wheat and bring it into my barn.'"

Understanding the Teaching

This parable describes a man who plants good seed in his field. An enemy sows weeds among the wheat under the cover of night. When the wheat and weeds both sprout, the man's servants are confused and consider removing weeds. The man advises against this to prevent harming the wheat. His strategy is to allow both to grow until harvest, at which time the reapers will sort them –burning the weeds and storing the wheat.

Key Points

1. **Good and Evil Coexist**
   This parable illustrates that good (represented by wheat) and evil (represented by weeds) will coexist in the world until the end times. This coexistence is a fundamental aspect of human experience and the spiritual realm.
2. **Enemy's Work**
   The enemy who sows the weeds, is a metaphor for the devil's influence in the world, causing sin and corruption.
3. **Patience and Discernment**
   The farmer's decision to let both grow together highlights the need for patience and discernment in dealing with evil.
4. **Final Judgment**
   The harvest symbolizes the final judgment when God will separate the righteous from the wicked.
5. **The Fate of the Righteous and Wicked**
   Just as the weeds are collected and burned, the wicked will face judgment. The wheat, representing the righteous, will be gathered into God's kingdom.

Exercises to Apply This Teaching

1. **Discernment in Judgment**
   Reflect on areas in life where you might be quick to judge. Practice patience and discernment, recognizing that final judgment is God's responsibility.
2. **Identify Weeds and Wheat**
   In your life, identify elements that represent weeds and wheat. Focus on nurturing the wheat and managing the weeds without harming the good.

3. **Study of Judgment**
   Study biblical teachings on judgment and the end times to gain a deeper understanding of this parable's implications.
4. **Prayer for Patience**
   Pray for patience and wisdom to coexist with the challenges and weeds in your community, workplace, or church.
5. **Share Insights**
   Share the parable with others and discuss its meaning and relevance in today's world, encouraging mutual understanding and patience.

Conclusion

The Parable of the Weeds teaches us about the complex reality of good and evil in the world. It encourages believers to practice discernment and patience, acknowledging that only God can rightfully judge and separate the righteous from the wicked. This parable reassures us of God's ultimate control over good and evil and reminds us of the impending judgment that awaits all creation.

Theologians' Take

Theologians view this parable as a lesson in theodicy, which involves the vindication of divine goodness and power in a world where evil is present. It's seen as an explanation of why God allows evil to exist alongside good and a warning against premature judgment. The parable is often discussed in the context of eschatology, the study of the end times, underlining the belief in a final judgment when God will righteously judge all. Theologians emphasize that this parable calls for faithful living in a complex world, trusting in God's ultimate justice and plan.

Chapter 42 – The Parables of the Mustard Seed and Yeast: Symbols of Growth and Influence

In Matthew 13:31-34, Jesus presents the Parables of the Mustard Seed and the Yeast, both of which illustrate how the kingdom of Heaven grows and influences.

"He told them another parable: 'The kingdom of heaven is like a mustard seed, which a man took and planted in his field. Though it is the smallest of all seeds, yet when it grows, it is the largest of garden plants and becomes a tree, so that the birds come and perch in its branches.'

He told them still another parable: 'The kingdom of heaven is like yeast that a woman took and mixed into about sixty pounds of flour until it worked all through the dough.'

Jesus spoke all these things to the crowd in parables; he did not say anything to them without using a parable. So was fulfilled what was spoken through the prophet:

'I will open my mouth in parables, I will utter things hidden since the creation of the world.'"

Understanding the Teaching:

Jesus compares the kingdom of Heaven to a mustard seed; one of the smallest seeds that grows into a large tree. He also likens it to yeast that a woman mixes into a large amount of flour until it works all through the dough.

These parables convey the idea of small beginnings leading to significant outcomes and the pervasive nature of the kingdom's influence.

Key Points:

1. **Small Beginnings, Significant Impact**
   The mustard seed, despite its small size, grows into a large tree. This symbolizes the kingdom of Heaven as a place that starts small but grows lavishly.
2. **Pervasive Influence**
   The yeast mixed into flour represents the kingdom's subtle but pervasive influence, transforming from within.
3. **Universal Reach**
   Both parables suggest that the kingdom of heaven will extend its influence far and wide beyond initial expectations.
4. **Organic Growth**
   The growth of the seed and the spreading of the yeast are natural processes, indicating the organic and unstoppable growth of God's kingdom.
5. **Hidden Work**
   The working of yeast in dough is mostly unseen, similar to how the kingdom of heaven often works in hidden but powerful ways.

Exercises to Apply This Teaching:

1. **Reflect on Small Beginnings**
   Identify small beginnings in your life that have the potential for significant spiritual growth. Invest time and effort into nurturing them.
2. **Be an Influence**
   Like yeast in dough, seek to influence your surroundings positively. This could be in your family, workplace, or community.

3. **Study Organic Growth**
   Study a plant or bake bread to understand the natural processes of growth and transformation. Reflect on how this relates to spiritual growth.
4. **Encourage Others**
   Encourage someone who feels their efforts are too small to be significant. Share the parables to inspire hope and persistence.
5. **Pray for Growth**
   Regularly pray for the growth of God's kingdom in your life and in the world. Ask for guidance on how you can contribute to this growth.

Conclusion

The Parables of the Mustard Seed and Yeast teach us about the kingdom of Heaven's humble beginnings and its expansive and transformative nature. These stories encourage believers to appreciate the small starts and the subtle workings of God's kingdom, which ultimately yield significant and far-reaching impacts.

Theologians' Take

Theologians interpret these parables as the way God's kingdom grows and spreads. The mustard seed and yeast are seen as metaphors on how the Gospel starts small but expands to reach all nations. Theologians also note the organic and almost mysterious nature of this growth, emphasizing that the kingdom operates on principles different from worldly power and influence. The kingdom's growth is understood as both a present reality and a future hope.

Chapter 43 – The Parables of the Hidden Treasure and the Pearl: Discovering Incomparable Value

In Matthew 13:44-46, Jesus presents two parables – the Hidden Treasure and the Pearl of Great Price. These parables illustrate the incomparable value of the kingdom of Heaven and the commitment it demands.

"The kingdom of heaven is like treasure hidden in a field. When a man found it, he hid it again, and then in his joy went and sold all he had and bought that field.

Again, the kingdom of heaven is like a merchant looking for fine pearls. When he found one of great value, he went away and sold everything he had and bought it."

Understanding the Teaching

The parable of the Hidden Treasure describes a man who finds a treasure hidden in a field. In his excitement, he hides it again and sells everything that he has in order to buy that field. Similarly, the Pearl of Great Price is about a merchant seeking fine pearls. Ultimately when he finds one, he goes on to sell everything that he has in order to buy it.

Key Points

1. **Incomparable Value**
   Both parables emphasize the supreme worth of the kingdom of Heaven.
2. **Joyful Discovery**
   The discovery of the treasure and the pearl brings great joy, symbolizing the joy found in the kingdom.

3. **Total Commitment**
   The characters in both parables sell all they have to possess the treasure, indicating the level of commitment required to follow Jesus.
4. **Active Search**
   The merchant actively searches for pearls, showing that seeking the kingdom is a deliberate and intentional pursuit.
5. **Willing Sacrifice**
   The willingness to give up everything else for the kingdom shows that its value surpasses all other worldly possessions or pursuits.

Exercises to Apply This Teaching

1. **Assess Your Values**
   Reflect on what you value most in life. Are these things in alignment with the values of the kingdom of Heaven?
2. **Joyful Discovery**
   Journal about a time when you experienced great joy in your spiritual journey. Reflect on how this mirrors the discovery of the kingdom's value.
3. **Prioritize the Kingdom**
   Identify one area of your life where the kingdom of heaven needs to take precedence. Make a plan to adjust your priorities accordingly.

4. **Active Pursuit**
   Set aside time each day to actively seek understanding and growth in your spiritual life through prayer, study, and meditation.
5. **Sacrificial Living**
   Consider what you might need to 'sell' or give up to embrace the kingdom of Heaven fully. Commit to making one change that reflects this.

Conclusion

The Parables of the Hidden Treasure and the Pearl of Great Price teach us about the unparalleled value of the kingdom of Heaven. They challenge us to recognize its worth, joyfully embrace it, and commit wholeheartedly to it, prioritizing it above everything else.

Theologians' Take

Theologians interpret these parables as a depiction of the radical nature of discipleship and the transformative power of encountering the kingdom. They highlight the joy and willingness depicted in the parables as essential attitudes in the Christian journey. Theologians also discuss the cost of discipleship, emphasizing that the kingdom of heaven, while a gift, demands a response that may cost everything else, yet is worth far more than its price.

Chapter 44 – The Parable of the Net: Understanding Final Judgment and Response

In Matthew 13:47-58, Jesus presents the Parable of the Net, an allegory illustrating the final judgment and the mixed reception of Jesus' teachings.

See the passage at the end of the Chapter

Understanding the Teaching

The parable describes a net thrown into the sea that catches fish of every kind. When it is full, fishermen pull it up, sit down, and collect the good fish in baskets. However, the bad fish are thrown away. Jesus explains that this is like the end of the age, where angels will separate the wicked from the righteous. The passage then narrates Jesus' return to his hometown, where he teaches in the synagogue, but the people are offended and do not believe in him.

Key Points

1. **Final Judgment**
   The net represents the kingdom of Heaven, gathering all people. The separation of fish signifies the final judgment, distinguishing the righteous from the wicked.
2. **Inevitable Sorting**
   Just as the net gathers all types of fish, the kingdom is open to all, but a final sorting is inevitable.

3. **Rejection of Jesus**
   The townspeople's offense at Jesus' wisdom and miraculous deeds reflects a lack of faith and understanding.

4. **Familiarity and Unbelief**
   Jesus notes a prophet is not honored in his own town, illustrating how familiarity can lead to unbelief.
5. **The Role of Faith**
   The passage suggests that Jesus did not do many miracles there because of their lack of faith, highlighting the importance of belief in receiving God's grace.

Exercises to Apply This Teaching

1. **Reflect on Judgment**
   Reflect on your own life in the light of the final judgment. Are you living in a way that reflects the values of the kingdom of Heaven?
2. **Openness to All**
   Consider how you can be more inclusive and loving in your community, mirroring the net that gathers all kinds of fish.
3. **Confront Familiarity**
   Identify any areas where familiarity might be blinding you to the truth. Seek to approach familiar aspects of your faith with fresh eyes and an open heart.
4. **Encourage Faith**
   Share your faith with others in a way that encourages belief and counters skepticism, especially with those familiar with Christianity but not committed.
5. **Faith in Action**
   Find a way to act on your faith every week in a tangible manner that demonstrates your commitment to living out the teachings of Jesus.

Conclusion

The Parable of the Net teaches us about the inclusive nature of the kingdom of Heaven and the reality of the final judgment. It challenges us to live our lives in a manner worthy of the kingdom, fully aware of the final separation that will occur. The passage also serves as a reminder of the importance of faith and the pitfalls of unbelief, even in familiar settings.

Theologians' Take

Theologians interpret the Parable of the Net as an eschatological warning, emphasizing the finality and inclusivity of God's judgment. The sorting of fish is often seen as symbolic of the end times when true righteousness will be distinguished from wickedness. Theologians also explore the theme of rejection and unbelief in Jesus' hometown, discussing how familiarity can sometimes hinder faith.

This part of the passage is often used to illustrate the importance of faith in Christ for the manifestation of God's power.

"Once again, the kingdom of heaven is like a net that was let down into the lake and caught all kinds of fish. When it was full, the fishermen pulled it up on the shore. Then they sat down and collected the good fish in baskets, but threw the bad away. This is how it will be at the end of the age. The angels will come and separate the wicked from the righteous and throw them into the blazing furnace, where there will be weeping and gnashing of teeth.

'Have you understood all these things?' Jesus asked. 'Yes,' they replied.

He said to them, 'Therefore every teacher of the law who has become a disciple in the kingdom of heaven is like the owner of a house who brings out of his storeroom new treasures as well as old.'

When Jesus had finished these parables, he moved on from there. Coming to his hometown, he began teaching the people in their synagogue, and they were amazed. 'Where did this man get this wisdom and these miraculous powers?' they asked. 'Isn't this the carpenter's son? Isn't his mother's name Mary, and aren't his brothers James, Joseph, Simon and Judas? Aren't all his sisters with us?

Where then did this man get all these things?' And they took offense at him. But Jesus said to them, 'A prophet is not without honor except in his own town and in his own home.'

And he did not do many miracles there because of their lack of faith."

Chapter 45 – Understanding "That Which Defiles"

In Matthew chapter 15 verses 1-20, Jesus addresses the concept of true purity and defilement. This challenges traditional religious notions and emphasizes inner righteousness over external rituals.

"Then some Pharisees and teachers of the law came to Jesus from Jerusalem and asked, 'Why do your disciples break the tradition of the elders? They don't wash their hands before they eat!'"

"Jesus replied, 'And why do you break the command of God for the sake of your tradition? For God said, 'Honor your father and mother' and 'Anyone who curses their father or mother is to be put to death.' But you say that if anyone declares that what might have been used to help their father or mother is 'devoted to God,' they are not to 'honor their father or mother' with it. Thus you nullify the word of God for the sake of your tradition. You hypocrites! Isaiah was right when he prophesied about you:

'These people honor me with their lips, but their hearts are far from me. They worship me in vain; their teachings are merely human rules.'"

"Jesus called the crowd to him and said, 'Listen and understand. What goes into someone's mouth does not defile them, but what comes out of their mouth, that is what defiles them.'"

"Then the disciples came to him and asked, 'Do you know that the Pharisees were offended when they heard this?' He replied, 'Every plant that my heavenly Father has not planted will be pulled up by the roots. Leave them; they are blind guides. If the blind lead the blind, both will fall into a pit.'"

"Peter said, 'Explain the parable to us.' 'Are you still so dull?' Jesus asked them. 'Don't you see that whatever enters the mouth goes into the stomach and then out of the body? But the things that come out of a person's mouth come from the heart, and these defile them. For out of the heart come evil thoughts—murder, adultery, sexual immorality, theft, false testimony, slander. These are what defile a person; but eating with unwashed hands does not defile them.'"

Understanding the Teaching

Pharisees and teachers of the law question Jesus about His disciples breaking the tradition of the elders by not washing their hands before eating. Jesus counters by questioning their own practices that violate God's commandments. He explains that what goes into someone's mouth does not defile them, but what comes out of their mouth, from their heart, is what defiles them. This teaching shifts the focus from external purity rituals to the condition of the heart and the importance of inner righteousness.

Key Points

1. **Inner Righteousness vs. External Rituals**
   Jesus emphasizes that true purity is a matter of the heart, not just adherence to external rituals.
2. **Hypocrisy of the Pharisees**
   He criticizes the Pharisees for their hypocrisy, where they upheld traditions but neglected the more critical matters of the law, like justice, mercy, and faithfulness.
3. **Source of Defilement**
   Jesus teaches that defilement comes from within, from the heart's evil thoughts, and is expressed through words and actions.
4. **Redefining Purity**
   This teaching redefines purity and holiness as a matter of inner transformation rather than mere ritual observance.

5. **Priority of God's Commandments**
   Jesus highlights the importance of prioritizing God's commandments over human traditions.

Exercises to Apply This Teaching

1. **Self-Reflection on Heart Condition**
   Reflect on your own heart and thoughts. Are there areas in your life where you prioritize outward appearances over inner righteousness?
2. **Challenge Hypocrisy**
   Identify any practices in your life that might be more about tradition than genuine faith. Consider ways to align your practices more closely with God's commandments.
3. **Practice Inner Purity**
   Engage in activities that foster inner purity, such as prayer, meditation, and reading scripture, focusing on themes of humility, love, and compassion.
4. **Community Discussion**
   Have a discussion in your community or church group about the difference between external rituals and inner righteousness.
5. **Acts of Mercy and Justice**
   Undertake an act of mercy or justice this week, reflecting on how such actions are expressions of true inner purity.

Conclusion

This passage teaches us that true defilement is not about what we consume or external rituals we follow, but about the condition of our hearts and the words and actions that flow from it. Jesus calls for a deeper understanding of purity, one that emphasizes inner transformation and aligns with God's commandments.

Theologians' Take

Theologians view this passage as a critique of legalistic religion that focuses on external rituals rather than heart transformation. They often discuss how Jesus reorients the concept of purity from ritual cleanliness to moral and ethical behavior. This passage is seen as an invitation to a deeper, more authentic faith that values inner righteousness over outward religious observance.

Chapter 46 – Understanding Jesus' Prediction of His Death

In Matthew 16:24-28, Jesus speaks about the cost of discipleship and His impending death, offering profound insights into self-denial and the nature of true followership.

"Then Jesus said to his disciples, 'Whoever wants to be my disciple must deny themselves and take up their cross and follow me. For whoever wants to save their life will lose it, but whoever loses their life for me will find it. What good will it be for someone to gain the whole world, yet forfeit their soul? Or what can anyone give in exchange for their soul? For the Son of Man is going to come in his Father's glory with his angels, and then he will reward each person according to what they have done. Truly I tell you, some who are standing here will not taste death before they see the Son of Man coming in his kingdom.'"

Understanding the Teaching

Jesus instructs His disciples about the necessity of self-denial and taking up one's cross to follow Him. He emphasizes that whoever wants to save their life will lose it, but whoever loses their life for His sake will find it. He questions what good it would be for someone to gain the whole world yet forfeit their soul. Jesus also mentions the Son of Man's coming in His Father's glory and His rewarding of each person according to what they have done.

Key Points

1. **Self-Denial**
   To follow Jesus truly you need to deny yourself, symbolizing the need to put aside selfish ambitions and desires.

2. **Taking Up the Cross**
   This signifies willingly accepting the suffering and challenges that come with being a disciple of Christ.
3. **Paradox of Losing and Finding Life**
   Jesus teaches that true life is found not in self-preservation but in self-giving for His sake.
4. **Value of the Soul**
   Jesus stresses the incomparable value of the soul, suggesting that no earthly gain is worth the loss of one's destiny.
5. **Divine Judgment**
   The reference to the Son of Man's return and the accompanying judgment underscores the accountability of every individual's actions.

Exercises to Apply This Teaching

1. **Reflect on Self-Denial**
   Assess areas in your life where self-denial is needed to better follow Jesus. Commit to one specific change that reflects this.
2. **Embrace Your Cross**
   Identify a current challenge or suffering in your life. Contemplate how embracing this as your cross can deepen your discipleship.
3. **Evaluate Priorities**
   Reflect on what you value most. How do these priorities align with the pursuit of eternal life and spiritual fulfillment?
4. **Acts of Self-Giving**
   Engage in an act of service or sacrifice this week that reflects the principle of losing life to find it in Christ.
5. **Accountability Journal**
   Keep a journal of your daily actions, reflecting on how they contribute to or detract from your spiritual growth and readiness for divine judgment.

Conclusion

In this passage of Matthew 16:24-28, we are confronted with the demanding yet rewarding path of discipleship. Jesus invites us to a life of self-denial and cross-bearing, promising that true life and fulfillment are found in surrendering to Him. This passage calls for deep introspection about our values, priorities, and the ultimate significance of our choices.

Theologians' Take

Theologians interpret this passage as crucial to understanding Christian discipleship. The concept of taking up one's cross is seen as a call to radical discipleship, where following Jesus might lead to suffering, but ultimately to true life.

The paradoxical saying about losing and finding life is viewed as a fundamental principle of Christian ethics and soteriology (the study of salvation).

Theologians also emphasize the eschatological aspect of this teaching, noting the promise of the Son of Man's return and the accompanying judgment.

Chapter 47 – The Kingdom of Heaven: Understanding Humility and Responsibility

In Matthew 18:1-9, Jesus addresses His disciples' query about who is the greatest in the kingdom of Heaven, teaching profound lessons on humility, responsibility, and spiritual vigilance.

"At that time the disciples came to Jesus and asked, 'Who, then, is the greatest in the kingdom of heaven?' He called a little child to him, and placed the child among them. And he said:

'Truly I tell you, unless you change and become like little children, you will never enter the kingdom of heaven. Therefore, whoever takes the lowly position of this child is the greatest in the kingdom of heaven. And whoever welcomes one such child in my name welcomes me.

'If anyone causes one of these little ones—those who believe in me— to stumble, it would be better for them to have a large millstone hung around their neck and to be drowned in the depths of the sea. Woe to the world because of the things that cause people to stumble! Such things must come, but woe to the person through whom they come! If your hand or your eye causes you to stumble, cut it off and throw it away. It is better for you to enter life maimed or blind than to have two hands or two eyes and be thrown into the fire of hell.'"

Understanding the Teaching

The disciples wonder who is considered to be the greatest in Heaven and ask Jesus about it. Jesus responds by placing a child among them and explains that unless they become like a child – humble and dependent – they cannot enter Heaven. So, whoever humbles themselves like a child is the greatest in the kingdom. He warns against causing "little ones" who believe in Him to stumble, emphasizing the severe consequences for leading others into sin. Jesus also speaks about removing sources of temptation, even if they are as dear as a hand or an eye, to avoid spiritual downfall.

Key Points

1. **Necessity of Humility**
   Humility, exemplified by a child's innocence and dependence, is essential to be part of the kingdom of Heaven.
2. **Warning Against Leading Others Astray**
   Jesus emphasizes the responsibility of believers not to be a stumbling block to others, especially to those new or vulnerable in faith.
3. **Severity of Sin**
   The graphic language of cutting off a hand or eye symbolizes the seriousness of dealing with sin and temptation.
4. **Childlike Faith**
   The analogy of becoming like a child highlights the importance of simple, trusting faith and lowliness.
5. **Accountability and Vigilance**
   Believers are called to be vigilant about their actions and influences, understanding their impact on others and themselves.

Exercises to Apply This Teaching

1. **Cultivating Humility**
   Practice humility in your daily interactions. Reflect on situations where you can put others' needs above your own, emulating childlike humility.
2. **Role Model**
   As a believer, be mindful of your influence on others, especially those new to the faith. Commit to being a positive role model.

3. **Tackling Temptations**
   Identify personal temptations or sources of sin. Take
   concrete steps to address and remove these from your life.
4. **Faith Reflection**
   Spend time reflecting on the simplicity and trust of childlike
   faith. Consider how this perspective can deepen your
   spiritual understanding.
5. **Community Care**
   Engage in an act of service or care within your community or
   church, especially focusing on supporting those who are
   vulnerable or young in their faith journey.

Conclusion

Matthew 18:1-9 teaches us about the qualities necessary to enter and
be great in the kingdom of Heaven, highlighting humility and
responsibility. Jesus calls for a childlike faith, free from pride, and a
serious commitment to living a life that avoids causing others to
stumble.

Theologians' Take

Theologians focus on the counter-cultural nature of Jesus' teaching,
which upends traditional notions of greatness and power. The
emphasis on humility and childlikeness is seen as central to
Christian ethics and discipleship. The harsh language about dealing
with sin reflects the seriousness with which Jesus treats moral
integrity and the spiritual health of the community. The passage is
also seen as emphasizing the importance of caring for and protecting
the vulnerable in the faith community.

Chapter 48 – The Parable of the Wandering Sheep: Emphasizing God's Care for the Lost

In this passage of Matthew 18:10-14, Jesus shares the Parable of the Wandering Sheep, which offers insights into God's love for each individual, especially those who are lost or marginalized.

"See that you do not despise one of these little ones. For I tell you that their angels in heaven always see the face of my Father in heaven [a].

"What do you think? If a man owns a hundred sheep, and one of them wanders away, will he not leave the ninety-nine on the hills and go to look for the one that wandered off? And if he finds it, truly I tell you, he is happier about that one sheep than about the ninety-nine that did not wander off. In the same way your Father in heaven is not willing that any of these little ones should perish."

[a] Matthew 18:11 Some manuscripts include here the words of Luke 19:10.

Understanding the Teaching

Jesus begins by cautioning against looking down on the little ones, referring to believers who may seem insignificant or are new in faith. He then tells a parable about a shepherd who has a hundred sheep and goes looking for the one that wandered away, leaving the ninety-nine. When he finds the lost sheep, he rejoices more over it than over the ninety-nine that did not wander off. Jesus explains that in the same way, it is not the will of the Father that any of these little ones should perish.

Key Points

1. **Value of Every Individual**
   This parable tells God's immense care for every individual,
   especially those who are lost or have gone astray.
2. **God's Pursuit of the Lost**
   The shepherd's action of leaving the ninety-nine to find the
   one lost sheep signifies God's active pursuit of those who are
   lost.
3. **Rejoicing in Restoration**
   The joy over finding the lost sheep symbolizes the joy in
   heaven over one sinner who repents.
4. **Priority of the Vulnerable**
   The emphasis on not despising the little ones reflects God's
   priority for the vulnerable and marginalized.
5. **Divine Will for Salvation**
   The parable underscores that it is God's will for all to be
   saved and not for any to be lost.

Exercises to Apply This Teaching

1. **Reflect on Individual Value**
   Meditate on your own value to God, especially if you ever
   feel lost or insignificant.
2. **Seek the Lost**
   Identify someone in your life who might be feeling 'lost' or
   distant from God. Find a way to reach out and offer support
   or encouragement.
3. **Celebrate Restoration**
   In your community or church, celebrate instances of
   individuals turning or returning to faith, recognizing the joy
   it brings to heaven.
4. **Advocate for the Vulnerable**
   Actively seek ways to support and advocate for the
   vulnerable or marginalized in your community.

5. **Pray for the Lost**
   Regularly pray for those who are spiritually lost, asking for their restoration and for guidance on how you can play a role in it.

Conclusion

The Parable of the Wandering Sheep teaches us about the boundless love of God for each of His children, His relentless pursuit of the lost, and the joy that accompanies their return. It challenges us to recognize the value of every person in God's eyes and to reflect this in our actions and attitudes.

Theologians' Take

Theologians interpret this parable as a representation of God's grace, highlighting His active role in seeking and saving the lost. It is seen as a reflection of the pastoral heart of God and His desire for redemption. Theologians also note the communal aspect, emphasizing the importance of community in seeking and caring for those who are lost or marginalized.

Chapter 49 – The Parable of the Unmerciful Servant: Understanding Forgiveness and Compassion

In the book of Matthew chapter 18 verses 22-35, Jesus conveys a crucial lesson on forgiveness through the Parable of the Unmerciful Servant, emphasizing the importance of showing mercy as we have received mercy.

See the entire passage at the end of the chapter.

Understanding the Teaching

After Peter asks Jesus about the limits of forgiveness, Jesus tells a parable about a king who wishes to settle accounts with his servants. One servant, unable to pay a massive debt, pleads for mercy. The king compassionately cancels the debt. However, this servant then refuses to show similar mercy to a fellow servant who owes him a much smaller amount, having him imprisoned for his inability to pay. When the king learns of this, he rebukes the unmerciful servant for not extending the mercy he himself had received and reinstates his original debt as punishment.

Key Points

1. **Infinite Forgiveness**
   Jesus suggests that forgiveness should not be limited but extended continually.
2. **Mercy Received, Mercy Given**
   This parable tells the expectation that those who have received mercy should similarly extend mercy to others.

3. **Severity of Unforgiveness**
   The harsh treatment of the unmerciful servant by the king underlines the seriousness with which God views the refusal to forgive others.
4. **Proportions of Debt**
   The enormous debt forgiven by the king represents our own debt of sin before God, while the smaller debt symbolizes the offenses we experience from others.
5. **Divine and Human Forgiveness**
   The parable connects our forgiveness of others with the forgiveness we receive from God.

Exercises to Apply This Teaching

1. **Reflect on Forgiveness**
   Consider if there's someone you need to forgive. Reflect on the mercy you've received from God and how you can extend that to others.
2. **Journaling Exercise**
   Write about a time you struggled to forgive someone and how you overcame it, or write about what's currently hindering you from offering forgiveness.
3. **Act of Reconciliation**
   If possible, reach out to someone you've wronged or who has wronged you to seek or offer forgiveness.
4. **Prayer for a Forgiving Heart**
   Regularly pray for a heart that is quick to forgive, asking God to help you let go of grudges and bitterness.
5. **Community Discussion**
   Engage in a discussion within your faith community about the challenges and importance of forgiveness.

Conclusion

The Parable of the Unmerciful Servant teaches the critical importance of forgiving others, reflecting the boundless mercy we have received from God. It challenges us to practice genuine forgiveness, recognizing that our willingness to forgive impacts our own experience of God's forgiveness.

Theologians' Take

Theologians discuss this parable in the context of the Christian virtue of forgiveness, emphasizing it as a fundamental aspect of Christian ethics and discipleship. The disproportionate debts are seen as highlighting God's grace in comparison to the relatively minor offenses we endure from others. The parable is also interpreted as illustrating the reciprocal nature of divine and human forgiveness, with a focus on the transformative power of mercy and the dangers of an unforgiving heart.

Jesus answered, "I tell you, not seven times, but seventy-seven times. Therefore, the kingdom of heaven is like a king who wanted to settle accounts with his servants. As he began the settlement, a man who owed him ten thousand bags of gold was brought to him. Since he was not able to pay, the master ordered that he and his wife and his children and all that he had be sold to repay the debt."

"At this the servant fell on his knees before him. 'Be patient with me,' he begged, 'and I will pay back everything.' The servant's master took pity on him, canceled the debt and let him go."

"But when that servant went out, he found one of his fellow servants who owed him a hundred silver coins. He grabbed him and began to choke him. 'Pay back what you owe me!' he demanded. His fellow servant fell to his knees and begged him, 'Be patient with me, and I will pay it back.'"

"But he refused. Instead, he went off and had the man thrown into prison until he could pay the debt. When the other servants saw what had happened, they were outraged and went and told their master everything that had happened."

"Then the master called the servant in. 'You wicked servant,' he said, 'I canceled all that debt of yours because you begged me to. Shouldn't you have had mercy on your fellow servant just as I had on you?' Shouldn't you have had mercy on your fellow servant just as had on you? In anger his master handed him over to the jailers to be tortured, until he should pay back all he owed. This is how my heavenly Father will treat each of you unless you forgive your brother or sister from your heart."

Chapter 50 – The Parable of the Workers in the Vineyard: Understanding God's Generosity

In Matthew 20:1-16, Jesus shares the Parable of the Workers in the Vineyard, offering insights into the nature of God's kingdom and His generosity.

See the Passage of Matthew 20: 1-16 at the end of the chapter.

Understanding the Teaching

This parable describes a landowner who hires workers for his vineyard to work during different hours throughout the day. Despite the difference in hours worked, he pays all the workers the same wage – a denarius, which he had initially agreed upon with the first group of workers. This action leads to discontent among those who worked all day, believing they should receive more. The landowner insists he is doing no wrong and is choosing to be generous with his money.

Key Points

1. **God's Generosity**
   The landowner's actions symbolize God's generosity. He gives not based on our merit or the length of service but out of His grace.
2. **Equality in God's Kingdom**
   The parable illustrates that all who come to God receive the same grace, regardless of their life's timing or duration in faith.
3. **Human Notions of Fairness**
   The disgruntled workers represent a human perspective of fairness, contrasting with God's ways.

4. **Sovereignty of God**
   The landowner's right to do what he wants with his money reflects God's sovereignty in dispensing His grace.
5. **The Last Will Be First**
   The concluding line, "the last will be first, and the first will be last," highlights the reversal of expectations in God's kingdom.

Exercises to Apply This Teaching

1. **Reflect on Grace**
   Reflect on your own life and consider how God's grace has been generously extended to you, regardless of your 'work' or 'merit.'
2. **Challenge Entitlement**
   Identify areas in your life where you might feel entitled to more from God. Pray for a heart that appreciates His grace.
3. **Embrace Humility**
   Practice humility, recognizing that others are also recipients of God's grace, irrespective of their background or life journey.
4. **Share the Parable**
   Share this parable with others and discuss its implications on how we view fairness, grace, and God's generosity.
5. **Serve Others Graciously**
   Engage in an act of service without expecting anything in return, reflecting the generous spirit of the landowner.

Conclusion

The Parable of the Workers in the Vineyard teaches us about the generous nature of God's kingdom. It challenges our conventional understanding of fairness, encouraging us to embrace God's grace that is freely given to all, regardless of their starting point in the journey of faith.

Theologians' Take

Theologians interpret this parable as a commentary on the last being first in the kingdom of Heaven. It is viewed as a narrative that breaks down human constructs of merit and reward, instead highlighting God's sovereign and gracious nature. The parable is also seen as a reassurance to latecomers to faith that they receive the same grace as those who have been faithful for longer.

"For the Kingdom of Heaven is like a landowner who went out early in the morning to hire workers for his vineyard. He agreed to pay them a denarius for the day and sent them into his vineyard. About nine in the morning he went out and saw others standing in the marketplace doing nothing. He told them, 'You also go and work in my vineyard, and I will pay you whatever is right.' So they went."

"He went out again about noon and about three in the afternoon and did the same thing. About five in the afternoon he went out and found still others standing around. He asked them, 'Why have you been standing here all day long doing nothing?' 'Because no one has hired us,' they answered. He said to them, 'You also go and work in my vineyard.'"

"When evening came, the owner of the vineyard said to his foreman, 'Call the workers and pay them their wages, beginning with the last ones hired and going on to the first.'"

"The workers who were hired about five in the afternoon came and each received a denarius. So when those came who were hired first, they expected to receive more. But each one of them also received a denarius. When they received it, they began to grumble against the landowner. 'These who were hired last worked only one hour,' they said, 'and you have made them equal to us who have borne the burden of the work and the heat of the day.'

"But he answered one of them, 'I am not being unfair to you, friend. Didn't you agree to work for a denarius? Take your pay and go. I want to give the one who was hired last the same as I gave you. Don't I have the right to do what I want with my own money? Or are you envious because I am generous?' So the last will be first, and the first will be last."

Chapter 51 – The Parable of the Two Sons: Understanding Obedience and Repentance

In Matthew 21:28-32, Jesus tells the Parable of the Two Sons, which emphasizes the importance of obedience and repentance to God.

"What do you think? There was a man who had two sons. He went to the first and said, 'Son, go and work today in the vineyard.' 'I will not,' he answered, but later he changed his mind and went. Then the father went to the other son and said the same thing. He answered, 'I will, sir,' but he did not go."

" 'Which of the two did what his father wanted?' 'The first,' they answered. Jesus said to them, 'Truly I tell you, the tax collectors and the prostitutes are entering the kingdom of God ahead of you. For John came to you to show you the way of righteousness, and you did not believe him, but the tax collectors and the prostitutes did. And even after you saw this, you did not repent and believe him.'"

Understanding the Teaching

This parable tells us about a man who had two sons. He asked both his sons work in his vineyard. The first son initially refused but later changed his mind and went to work while the second son, who agreed to go, did not. Jesus used this parable to highlight the difference between saying and doing God's will, emphasizing that true obedience is in actions, not just words.

Key Points

1. **Actions vs. Words**
   The parable tells us that actions speak louder than words when it comes to God's obedience.

2. **Repentance and Change**
   The first son's change of mind and subsequent action
   represent true repentance and obedience.
3. **Hypocrisy Exposed**
   The second son's failure to fulfill his promise exposes the
   hypocrisy of professing commitment to God but failing to act
   accordingly.
4. **Judgment on Religious Leaders**
   Jesus uses the parable to critique the religious leaders of His
   time, who, like the second son, did not live up to their words.
5. **Acceptance of Sinners**
   The parable suggests that sinners who repent and obey God
   are more pleasing to Him than the self-righteous who only
   pay lip service.

Exercises to Apply This Teaching

1. **Self-Reflection**
   Reflect on areas in your life where your actions may not
   align with your words. Commit to aligning your actions
   more closely with your professed beliefs.
2. **Act on Commitments**
   Identify a commitment you've made but have yet to fulfill.
   Take a concrete step to act on it.
3. **Study on Repentance**
   Spend time studying biblical teachings on repentance.
   Reflect on how these teachings can be applied in your life.
4. **Prayer for Integrity**
   Regularly pray for the integrity to follow through on your
   commitments and for the courage to change your mind and
   actions when necessary.
5. **Community Service**
   Engage in a community service activity as a practical way to
   demonstrate your commitment to living out your faith.

Conclusion

The Parable of the Two Sons teaches us about the importance of genuine repentance and the need to follow through on our commitments to God with actions, not just words. It challenges us to examine our lives for areas of inconsistency and to strive for true obedience to God's will.

Theologians' Take

Theologians view this parable as a commentary on religious complacency and the transformative power of repentance. It's seen as a call to authentic discipleship, emphasizing the need for a life that reflect one's faith. Theologians note that the parable was directed at religious leaders to challenge their superficial adherence to religious practices without genuine heart change.

Chapter 52 – The Parable of the Tenants: Understanding Stewardship and Judgment

In Matthew 21:33-43, Jesus narrates the Parable of the Tenants, conveying deep insights into stewardship, accountability, and the consequences of rejecting God's messengers.

See the Passage of Matthew 21:33-43 at the end of the chapter.

Understanding the Teaching

This parable tells of a landowner who plants a vineyard, equips it with everything needed, and then leases it to tenants before going on a journey. When harvest time approaches, he sends his servants to collect his share of the fruit, but the tenants beat, kill, and stone the servants. Finally, he sends his son, thinking they will respect him, but the tenants kill the son to seize his inheritance. Jesus concludes by saying that the kingdom of God will be taken away from those who don't produce its fruits and given to others who will.

Key Points

1. **God's Provision and Expectation**
   The landowner represents God, who provides everything (the vineyard) and expects stewardship and fruits in return.
2. **Rejection of Prophets**
   The tenants' mistreatment of the servants symbolizes the leaders of Israel's rejection of God's prophets.

3. **Christ's Rejection and Sacrifice**
   The killing of the son represents the rejection and crucifixion of Jesus.

4. **Judgment and Transfer of Privilege**
   The landowner's judgment on the tenants signifies the transfer of the kingdom of God to those who will produce its fruits.
5. **Responsibility of Stewardship**
   The parable emphasizes the responsibility that comes with being entrusted with God's work.

Exercises to Apply This Teaching

1. **Reflect on Stewardship**
   Reflect on how you are stewarding the gifts and responsibilities God has given you. Are you producing fruit that aligns with God's purpose?
2. **Study Biblical Prophets**
   Study the lives of biblical prophets to understand their messages and how they were received.
3. **Gratitude for Christ's Sacrifice**
   Spend time in prayer or meditation, reflecting on the sacrifice of Christ and what it means for your life.
4. **Community Contribution**
   Actively seek ways to contribute positively to your faith community, ensuring that you are helping it produce kingdom fruits.
5. **Discuss Accountability**
   Have a discussion in your church or study group about the parable's themes of stewardship, accountability, and judgment.

Conclusion

The Parable of the Tenants teaches about the grave consequences of rejecting God's messengers and failing to fulfill our role as stewards of His kingdom. It underscores the need for accountability and the righteous judgment that follows unfaithfulness. The parable also emphasizes the religious leaders' failure to recognize and accept

God's messengers and the coming of the kingdom of God. It also alludes to the transfer of the kingdom from the religious leaders to others who would produce its fruit.

Theologians' Take

Theologians interpret this parable as an allegory of God's dealings with Israel and the emerging Christian church. The rejection of the son is seen as foretelling Jesus' own rejection and death, and the transfer of the vineyard signifies the opening of the kingdom of God to all, including Gentiles.

The parable is discussed in the context of divine judgment, the responsibility of religious leaders, and the broader theme of God's faithfulness despite human unfaithfulness.

"Listen to another parable: There was a landowner who planted a vineyard. He put a wall around it, dug a winepress in it and built a watchtower. Then he rented the vineyard to some farmers and moved to another place. When the harvest time approached, he sent his servants to the tenants to collect his fruit."

"The tenants seized his servants; they beat one, killed another, and stoned a third. Then he sent other servants to them, more than the first time, and the tenants treated them the same way. Last of all, he sent his son to them. 'They will respect my son,' he said."

"But when the tenants saw the son, they said to each other, 'This is the heir. Come, let's kill him and take his inheritance.' So they took him and threw him out of the vineyard and killed him. Therefore, when the owner of the vineyard comes, what will he do to those tenants?"

"He will bring those wretches to a wretched end," they replied, "and he will rent the vineyard to other tenants, who will give him his share of the crop at harvest time."

Jesus said to them, "Have you never read in the Scriptures:

'The stone the builders rejected

has become the cornerstone;

the Lord has done this,

and it is marvelous in our eyes'?

Therefore I tell you that the kingdom of God will be taken away from you and given to a people who will produce its fruit. He who falls on this stone will be broken to pieces, but he on whom it falls will be crushed."

Chapter 53 – The Parable of the Wedding Banquet: Understanding God's Invitation and Response

In Matthew 22:1-14, Jesus shares the Parable of the Wedding Banquet and highlighting the nature of God's invitation to His kingdom and the varied responses it elicits.

Jesus spoke to them again in parables, saying: "The kingdom of heaven is like a king who prepared a wedding banquet for his son. He sent his servants to those who had been invited to the banquet to tell them to come, but they refused to come.

"Then he sent some more servants and said, 'Tell those who have been invited that I have prepared my dinner: My oxen and fattened cattle have been butchered, and everything is ready. Come to the wedding banquet.'

"But they paid no attention and went off—one to his field, another to his business. The rest seized his servants, mistreated them and killed them. The king was enraged. He sent his army and destroyed those murderers and burned their city.

"Then he said to his servants, 'The wedding banquet is ready, but those I invited did not deserve to come. So go to the street corners and invite to the banquet anyone you find.' So the servants went out into the streets and gathered all the people they could find, the bad as well as the good, and the wedding hall was filled with guests.

"But when the king came in to see the guests, he noticed a man there who was not wearing wedding clothes. He asked, 'How did you get in here without wedding clothes, friend?' The man was speechless.

"Then the king told the attendants, 'Tie him hand and foot, and throw him outside, into the darkness, where there will be weeping and gnashing of teeth.'

"For many are invited, but few are chosen."

Understanding the Teaching

This parable narrates a king who arranges a wedding banquet for his son. He sends servants to call those invited, but they refuse to come. He sends more servants, detailing the prepared feast, yet the invitees ignore the call, mistreat the servants, and even kill some. The king, in anger, destroys the murderers and their city. Then, he instructs his servants to invite anyone they find. The hall is filled with guests, but the king sees a man without wedding clothes and has him thrown out for not being dressed appropriately, concluding with the statement, "For many are invited, but few are chosen."

Key Points

1. **Universal Invitation**
    The king's invitation to everyone signifies God's offer of salvation to all people, not just a select few.
2. **Rejection and Indifference**
    The initial invitees' refusal represents those who reject God's invitation due to indifference or preoccupation with worldly matters.
3. **Consequences of Rejection**
    The severe reaction of the king to those who mistreat his servants symbolizes the judgment awaiting those who reject God and mistreat His messengers.

4. **Requirement for Righteousness**
    The guest without wedding clothes represents the need for righteousness (symbolized by appropriate attire) to partake in God's kingdom.

5. **Selective Acceptance**
   The concluding statement underscores that while God's invitation is broad, acceptance into His kingdom is conditional on the proper response.

Exercises to Apply This Teaching

1. **Reflect on Your Response**
   Contemplate your response to God's invitation. Are you fully embracing it, or are there areas of indifference or rejection in your life?
2. **Share the Invitation**
   Share the message of God's invitation with someone who may not have heard it or may feel excluded from it.
3. **Examine Your Attire**
   Reflect on whether your life reflects the righteousness required to be part of God's kingdom. Identify areas for spiritual growth.
4. **Prayer for Readiness**
   Pray to be ready for God's kingdom, asking for guidance to live a life that aligns with His will.
5. **Discussion on Acceptance**
   Discuss in a group setting what it means to be 'chosen' and how this relates to faith and actions.

Conclusion

The Parable of the Wedding Banquet teaches about the inclusiveness of God's invitation to His kingdom and the importance of the right response to this call. It challenges us to examine our own acceptance of God's invitation and to live in a manner worthy of being part of His kingdom.

Theologians' Take

Theologians interpret this parable as a reflection of God's grace extending beyond Israel to the Gentiles. The rejection by the first invitees is seen as symbolic of Israel's rejection of Jesus, and the subsequent broad invitation symbolizes the opening of the kingdom to everyone. The removal of the improperly dressed guest is interpreted as the necessity of genuine faith and righteous living to enter into the kingdom.

Chapter 54 – The Parable of the Ten Virgins: Understanding Preparedness and Vigilance

In Matthew 25:1-13, Jesus tells the Parable of the Ten Virgins. He emphasizes the importance of being prepared and vigilant for kingdom come.

"At that time the kingdom of heaven will be like ten virgins who took their lamps and went out to meet the bridegroom. Five of them were foolish, and five were wise. The foolish ones took their lamps but did not take any oil with them. The wise ones, however, took oil in jars along with their lamps. The bridegroom was a long time in coming, and they all became drowsy and fell asleep.

"At midnight the cry rang out: 'Here's the bridegroom! Come out to meet him!'

"Then all the virgins woke up and trimmed their lamps. The foolish ones said to the wise, 'Give us some of your oil; our lamps are going out.'

"'No,' they replied, 'there may not be enough for both us and you. Instead, go to those who sell oil and buy some for yourselves.'

"But while they were on their way to buy the oil, the bridegroom arrived. The virgins who were ready went in with him to the wedding banquet, and the door was shut.

"Later the others also came. 'Lord, Lord,' they said, 'open the door for us!'

"But he replied, 'Truly I tell you, I don't know you.'

"Therefore keep watch, because you do not know the day or the hour."

Understanding the Teaching

This parable describes ten virgins who took their lamps and went to meet the bridegroom. Out of the ten, five were foolish who did not take oil with their lamps, while the others were wise and took oil in jars along with their lamps. When the bridegroom was late, all of them fell asleep. At midnight, there was a cry announcing the bridegroom's arrival. The foolish virgins asked the wise for oil, but there wasn't enough for all. While they went to buy oil, the bridegroom arrived, and those who were ready went in with him to the wedding banquet, and the door was shut. When the foolish virgins returned, they were not allowed in, emphasizing the need for readiness.

Key Points

1. **Preparation for Christ's Return**
   The parable underscores the necessity of being prepared for Christ's return, which can happen unexpectedly.
2. **Wisdom vs. Foolishness**
   The wise virgins symbolize those who are prepared for the kingdom of Heaven, while the foolish represent unpreparedness.
3. **Importance of Personal Preparedness**
   The refusal of the wise virgins to share their oil suggests that some aspects of faith and preparedness cannot be borrowed or acquired at the last minute.
4. **Readiness at All Times**
   The unexpected arrival of the bridegroom highlights the need to be vigilant and ready at all times.
5. **Consequences of Unpreparedness**
   The closed door for the foolish virgins shows the irreversible consequences of not being prepared.

Exercises to Apply This Teaching

1. **Personal Reflection on Preparedness**
   Reflect on your own spiritual preparedness. Are you living in a way that keeps you ready for Christ's return?
2. **Vigilance in Faith Practices**
   Commit to regular faith practices like prayer, Bible study, and fellowship to keep your spiritual life vigilant and active.
3. **Discussion on Readiness**
   Engage in a discussion with friends or a study group about what it means to be spiritually prepared.
4. **Prayer for Wisdom**
   Pray for wisdom and guidance to maintain vigilance and preparedness in your spiritual journey.
5. **Help Others Prepare**
   Find ways to encourage and help others in their journey of faith and preparedness for the Kingdom of Heaven.

Conclusion

The Parable of the Ten Virgins teaches the critical importance of being spiritually prepared and vigilant for the coming of Christ. It serves as a sobering reminder that readiness for God's kingdom is a personal responsibility with eternal consequences.

Theologians' Take

Theologians often interpret this parable in the context of eschatology, emphasizing the unpredictable timing of Christ's return and the need for constant vigilance. The parable is viewed as a call to active and ongoing spiritual preparedness, highlighting the personal nature of faith and the irrevocable consequences of being unprepared.

Chapter 55 – The Parable of the Bags of Gold: Understanding Stewardship and Accountability

In Matthew 25:14-30, Jesus tells the Parable of the Bags of Gold (also known as the Parable of the Talents), which focuses on the themes of stewardship, responsibility, and the use of God-given resources.

"Again, it will be like a man going on a journey, who called his servants and entrusted his wealth to them. To one he gave five bags of gold, to another two bags, and to another one bag, each according to his ability. Then he went on his journey. The man who had received five bags of gold went at once and put his money to work and gained five bags more. So also, the one with two bags of gold gained two more. But the man who had received one bag went off, dug a hole in the ground and hid his master's money."

"After a long time the master of those servants returned and settled accounts with them. The man who had received five bags of gold brought the other five. 'Master,' he said, 'you entrusted me with five bags of gold. See, I have gained five more.'"

"His master replied, 'Well done, good and faithful servant! You have been faithful with a few things; I will put you in charge of many things. Come and share your master's happiness!'

"The man with two bags of gold also came. 'Master,' he said, 'you entrusted me with two bags of gold; see, I have gained two more.'"

"His master replied, 'Well done, good and faithful servant! You have been faithful with a few things; I will put you in charge of many things. Come and share your master's happiness!'

"Then the man who had received one bag of gold came. 'Master,' he said, 'I knew that you are a hard man, harvesting where you have not sown and gathering where you have not scattered seed. So I was afraid and went out and hid your gold in the ground. See, here is what belongs to you.'"

"His master replied, 'You wicked, lazy servant! So you knew that I harvest where I have not sown and gather where I have not scattered seed? Well then, you should have put my money on deposit with the bankers, so that when I returned I would have received it back with interest."

"'So take the bag of gold from him and give it to the one who has ten bags. For whoever has will be given more, and they will have an abundance. Whoever does not have, even what they have will be taken from them. And throw that worthless servant outside, into the darkness, where there will be weeping and gnashing of teeth.'"

Understanding the Teaching

The parable describes a man going on a journey who entrusts his property to his servants. He gives the first servant five bags of gold; the second, two bags; and to third one bag, each according to their ability. The servants who had five and two bags of gold invested and doubled their money. However, the servant who had one bag hides his master's money in a hole. When the master returns, he commends the first two servants for their good work but rebukes and punishes the third for his laziness and failure to use the resources given to him.

Key Points

1. **Stewardship of Resources**
   This parable highlights the importance of wisely using the resources and talents God has entrusted to us.

2. **Differing Abilities**
   The varying amounts of money given to the servants indicate that people are entrusted with different resources and abilities.
3. **Accountability and Reward**
   The master's commendation of the first two servants shows that faithfulness in stewardship leads to reward.
4. **Consequences of Inaction**
   The punishment of the third servant underscores the consequences of inactivity and failure to utilize one's potential.
5. **God's Expectations**
   The parable teaches that God expects His followers to actively and effectively use what He has given them for the growth of His kingdom.

Exercises to Apply This Teaching

1. **Inventory of Talents**
   Reflect on the talents and resources you possess. Consider how you can better utilize them for God's purposes.
2. **Set a Goal**
   Set a specific, tangible goal to use one of your talents or resources to benefit others or contribute to your community.
3. **Learning and Growth**
   Engage in a new activity or learning experience that helps you develop a talent or better steward your resources.
4. **Accountability Partner**
   Find someone who can hold you accountable for utilizing your talents and resources effectively.
5. **Reflect on Inaction**
   Consider the consequences of inaction. Reflect on a time when you failed to use your talents and think about what you could do differently now.

Conclusion

The Parable of the Bags of Gold teaches the importance of actively using our God-given talents and resources. It challenges us to be faithful stewards, understanding that we will be held accountable for how we use what we have been given.

Theologians' Take

Theologians often discuss this parable in the context of stewardship and the Christian's responsibility to use their God-given gifts for the service of God and others. This parable is seen as emphasizing the active nature of faith and the expectation of productivity in the Christian life. It is also interpreted as a lesson on the responsible use of material and spiritual resources in anticipation of Christ's return.

Chapter 56 – The Parable of the Sheep and the Goats: Understanding Compassion and Judgment

In Matthew 25:31-46, Jesus presents the Parable of the Sheep and the Goats, a powerful teaching about the final judgment and the importance of compassionate action.

See the passage of Matthew 25:31-46 at the end of the chapter.

Understanding the Teaching

The passage depicts the Son of Man coming in glory and separating people as a shepherd separates sheep from goats. The sheep on the right are commended for their compassionate actions: feeding the hungry, welcoming the stranger, clothing the naked, caring for the sick, and visiting prisoners. They are told that by doing these things for the society, they did indirectly did them for Christ. Conversely, the goats on the left are reprimanded for failing to do these things and are sent away to eternal punishment, while the righteous enter eternal life.

Key Points

1. **Judgment Based on Actions**
   The separation of sheep and goats symbolizes the final judgment based on individuals' actions toward others.
2. **Serving Christ Through Others**
   Jesus teaches that serving those in need is equivalent to serving Him directly.
3. **Importance of Compassion**
   The criteria for judgment emphasize the importance of compassion and practical help for those in need.

4. **Responsibility to Act**
   The parable shows that followers of Christ have a responsibility to actively care for the vulnerable or marginalized.
5. **Eternal Consequences**
   This passage highlights the eternal consequences of one's actions, with the righteous receiving eternal life and the unrighteous with eternal punishment.

Exercises to Apply This Teaching

1. **Reflect on Compassionate Actions**
   Reflect on how your actions align with those commended in the parable. Identify ways to be more actively compassionate.
2. **Volunteer**
   Engage in a volunteer activity that helps meet the needs of the vulnerable in your community.
3. **Pray for Compassion**
   Regularly pray for a compassionate heart and for opportunities to serve Christ through serving others.
4. **Learn About Needs**
   Educate yourself about the needs in your community or globally and consider how you can contribute meaningfully.
5. **Share the Message**
   Share the message of this parable with others, encouraging them to reflect on their own actions and the call to serve Christ through serving others.

Conclusion

The Parable of the Sheep and the Goats teaches us about the importance of compassionate action and the reality of final judgment. It challenges us to see Christ in others, especially in the society we serve as we would serve Christ Himself.

Theologians' Take

Theologians discuss this parable in the context of Christian ethics and eschatology, emphasizing the essential role of ethical behavior in Christian life. The parable is seen as a call to social justice and the practical expression of faith through acts of mercy. It also emphasizes the reality of final judgment and the eternal consequences of our actions, reflecting the integral connection between faith and deeds in Christian theology.

"When the Son of Man comes in his glory, and all the angels with him, he will sit on his glorious throne. All the nations will be gathered before him, and he will separate the people one from another as a shepherd separates the sheep from the goats. He will put the sheep on his right and the goats on his left."

"Then the King will say to those on his right, 'Come, you who are blessed by my Father; take your inheritance, the kingdom prepared for you since the creation of the world. For I was hungry and you gave me something to eat, I was thirsty and you gave me something to drink, I was a stranger and you invited me in, I needed clothes and you clothed me, I was sick and you looked after me, I was in prison and you came to visit me.'"

"Then the righteous will answer him, 'Lord, when did we see you hungry and feed you, or thirsty and give you something to drink? When did we see you a stranger and invite you in, or needing clothes and clothe you? When did we see you sick or in prison and go to visit you?'"

"The King will reply, 'Truly I tell you, whatever you did for one of the least of these brothers and sisters of mine, you did for me.'

Then he will say to those on his left, 'Depart from me, you who are cursed, into the eternal fire prepared for the devil and his angels. For I was hungry and you gave me nothing to eat, I was thirsty and you gave me nothing to drink, I was a stranger and you did not invite me in, I needed clothes and you did not clothe me, I was sick and in prison and you did not look after me.'"

"They also will answer, 'Lord, when did we see you hungry or thirsty or a stranger or needing clothes or sick or in prison, and did not help you?' He will reply, 'Truly I tell you, whatever you did not do for one of the least of these, you did not do for me.' Then they will go away to eternal punishment, but the righteous to eternal life."

Chapter 57 – Conclusion of the Parables and Transition to the Passion of Christ

As we conclude our journey through the parables of Jesus in the Gospel of Matthew, we transition to a pivotal moment in the narrative: the betrayal, crucifixion, and ultimate sacrifice of Jesus Christ. This period marks the fulfillment of His mission on Earth, embodying profound expressions of forgiveness, sacrifice, and the human-divine connection.

Jesus' Profound Statements During His Crucifixion

Among the most poignant moments during the crucifixion is when Jesus, bearing immense pain, expresses forgiveness by saying,

"Forgive them, Father, for they know not what they do" (Luke 23:34).

This statement reflects the depth of Jesus' compassion, His commitment to forgiveness, and the fulfillment of His teaching on loving one's enemies.

In Matthew 27:46, Jesus makes another profound statement: "My God, my God, why have you forsaken me?" This cry, echoing Psalm 22, reveals the depth of Jesus' suffering and His profound human experience of abandonment. This moment of anguish highlights the true cost of our redemption and the extent of Jesus' sacrifice.

Passage - Matthew 27:46:

About three in the afternoon Jesus cried out in a loud voice, "Eli, Eli, lema sabachthani?" (which means "My God, my God, why have you forsaken me?").

Understanding Matthew 27:46

1. **Expression of Suffering**
   Jesus' words reflect His deep physical and emotional pain, embodying the fullness of human suffering.
2. **Identification with Humanity**
   In expressing feelings of abandonment, Jesus fully identifies with the human condition, experiencing the depths of human despair and alienation.
3. **Fulfillment of Scripture**
   This statement fulfills the prophetic Psalm 22, linking Jesus' suffering to the messianic predictions of the Old Testament.
4. **The Mystery of Divine Abandonment**
   Jesus' cry touches on the mystery of the cross where, in a moment, the Son feels separation from the Father, highlighting the seriousness of sin and the cost of salvation.

Conclusion

Jesus' crucifixion and His words during this time encapsulate the core of Christian faith the embodiment of divine love and forgiveness, even in the face of betrayal and suffering. His sacrifice on the cross and His cry of forsakenness bring to fruition His teachings and parables, offering salvation and hope to humanity.

Theologians' Take

Theologians discuss Jesus' cry from the cross as a profound theological mystery. It is seen as an expression of the genuine human experience of Jesus, underscoring the reality of His incarnation. This moment is also interpreted as a revelation of the profound spiritual burden of sin and the extreme separation it causes between humanity and God, which Jesus took upon Himself. Theologians view this as a pivotal moment in the redemptive work of Christ, symbolizing both the depth of human suffering and the height of divine love.

Closing Thoughts: Gratitude and Reflection on the Journey Through Matthew's Parables

As we close this enlightening journey through the book of Matthew, I extend my heartfelt gratitude to each one of you for joining me in exploring the depth and wisdom of Jesus' parables. Our expedition through these narratives has been more than an academic exercise; it has been a transformative experience, uncovering the profound truths hidden within these timeless stories.

Impactful Understanding and Lessons Discovered

Our journey has revealed the multifaceted nature of Jesus' teachings, each parable a gem offering insights into God's kingdom, human nature, and the path of righteousness. We've explored into the themes of forgiveness, compassion, preparedness, and stewardship, all intricately woven into the fabric of Jesus' teachings.

We discovered that the parables are not just ancient stories but living words that continue to challenge, inspire, and transform us. They call us to self-reflection, beckoning us to align our lives more closely with the principles of the kingdom of Heaven.

Conclusion Embracing the Teachings of Jesus

As we conclude, let us carry with us the profound lessons of humility, love, and mercy that Jesus so eloquently taught. Let these parables continue to resonate in our hearts and minds, guiding our actions and decisions.

Call to Action for the Readers

I urge you, dear readers, not to let this journey end here. Let the parables of Matthew be a catalyst for continual growth and exploration in your faith. Take these teachings into your communities, families, and daily lives. Let them inspire acts of kindness, moments of forgiveness, and a deeper commitment to living a life reflective of the values Jesus championed.

Engage in conversations about these parables with others, share the insights you have gained, and listen to the perspectives of others. Let the wisdom of Jesus' words be a light in your life, guiding you to live with purpose, love, and hope.

Finally, I encourage you to revisit these parables often, for in them, you will always find new treasures of wisdom waiting to be discovered. May your journey through the teachings of Jesus continue to enrich and transform your life!

Thank you for allowing me to share this journey with you. May you be blessed and guided by the enduring wisdom of the parables in the Gospel of Matthew and many more great profits/Prophets' writings throughout the New Testament from the greatest book that's ever written. *The Bible*.

Get in touch

www.ingramcontent.com/pod-product-compliance
Lightning Source LLC
Chambersburg PA
CBHW051149120626
46547CB00012B/1003